A TRIANGLE OF LAND

A History of the Site and the Founding
of Brookdale Community College

BROOKDALE

county college
of Monmouth

A TRIANGLE OF LAND

A History of the Site
and the Founding of
Brookdale Community College

The Northern Monmouth County Branch of
The American Association of University Women

Published by Brookdale Community College, Lincroft, N.J.

CONTENTS

FOREWORD

If you accept 1968 as "the beginning," Brookdale Community College is ten years old this year.

Being ten years old is not in itself much of an achievement . . . at least for a college. The ten tiny candles on Brookdale's cake flicker dimly indeed in the deep, ivy-hung shadows of our nation's older hallowed halls of learning.

Still, Brookdale has just cause to mark the occasion. Brookdale celebrates not the achievement of the great age of ten. Brookdale celebrates the dynamic new dimension the college has given to life in Monmouth County, New Jersey, in ten short, fast years. Brookdale celebrates the fruition of the idea of a few forward-thinking citizens to provide for all citizens a diversity and excellence of educational opportunity worthy of national recognition.

Brookdale is unique . . . a product of its community and, to a considerable degree, of its environment. The geographic and historic characteristics of Monmouth County, the 100-year-old barns in which the first students started, the rural beauty of Brookdale Farm, the memory of the strong-minded and public spirited Geraldine Thompson, even the Derby-winning filly named "Regret" who was bred and trained here . . . all have influenced the nature of Brookdale Community College.

Since ten years is such a short time in itself, and since some of the things that make Brookdale what it is go back ten times ten years and more . . . what better way to mark our tenth birthday than to publish a history of the "triangle of land" on which we stand today and of the people who lived on it and loved it before us?

In July, 1976, we enlisted the aid of the Northern Monmouth County Branch of the American Association of University Women . . . an organization that had played a key role in the establishment of the college and has maintained a significant volunteer relationship with Brookdale in numerous activities. We asked if they would research and write a history of Brookdale from early colonial times through the establishment of the college. Typical of AAUW, they tackled the project with the greatest enthusiasm and skill . . . and the end result is in your hands.

But it didn't get there easily! Hundreds of pages of notes were accumulated in researching archives and libraries. Fifty people related to the college and to the farm were interviewed and transcribed tapes ran to 1500 typewritten pages. In the fifteen months from inception of actual work to final edited manuscript, more than forty volunteers put in 3100 hours of work not counting typing time.

We can never adequately thank either the women of AAUW or the people of the community who gave their time so freely for the interviews. We can only hope that they will hear spontaneously from appreciative readers and thereby enjoy some small part of the recognition they deserve.

PHILIP C. CARLING
Executive Director, Public Affairs
Brookdale Community College

INTRODUCTION

For Brookdale Community College, the community is at the center of things. It has been that way since before the beginning.

It was community groups, led by the Northern Monmouth Branch of the American Association of University Women, which first held aloft the ideal of an independent institution to serve the community's diversity. That ideal became a community cause and the cause became a community's college. For the tenth anniversary of that college, a look backward seemed appropriate, but what form should it take?

The usual college history seeks to assure the old boys (and sometimes the girls) that all is as it was then, while simultaneously regaling prospective students with the modernity of it all. Such a history usually reposes in the slightly musty back stacks of The College Library, a few copies tucked into the bookshelves of alumni of generous inclination. An excerpt (complete with imitation rotogravure photos) is printed in the alumni magazine. The usual college history format held no relevance for the County College of Monmouth.

This history, written by members of the Northern Monmouth Branch of AAUW is that organization's response to a college need. It is one more example in a continuum of efforts on behalf of the college. It is a response by a community of writers and researchers, who undertook and saw to its conclusion a task which they now recognize "was much more difficult than we ever dreamed."

This history of the college, of the land where it stands and serves, and of the people who once lived there, represents, in the words of project director, Joan Grantges, "the community coming together to do something for the community."

I commend it to the reader because it is interesting reading in its own right and because it is one more example of what the community can do when it undertakes to work as a community.

ELINOR S. MULTER

THE AAUW COMMITTEE

Project Director:	Joan Grantges	
Editor-in-Chief:	Susan C. Kline	
Assistants to the Director:	Meline Karakashian Patricia Moran	Pauline Quackenbush Linda Lott Rizzo
Associate Editors:	Joan Grantges	Pauline Quackenbush
Assistant Editors:	Janet Cavanaugh Sharon Grantges Ann Kappel Carolyn Millhiser	Susan Nassau Ellen Prozeller Joyce Reeves Linda Lott Rizzo
Writers: Part I: *Part II:* *Part III:*	Dianne Petruzella Linda Lott Rizzo Joan Grantges	Linda Pollack Meline Karakashian Nancy Swann
Interviewers:	Joan Grantges Meline Karakashian Phyllis Lacka Ceil Langa Patricia Moran Madeline Muise	Kay O'Neill Pauline Quackenbush June Sallee Martha Thompson Marian Wattenbarger
Assistant Interviewers:	Janet Cavanaugh Carol Brady	Dianne Petruzella
Researchers:	Joan Donaldson Irene Gibson Joan Grantges Meline Karakashian Ellen Morris Susan Nassau	Dianne Petruzella Linda Pollack Linda Lott Rizzo Nancy Swann Ellen Tammaru
Research Assistants:	Pearl Bell Renee Brignola Florence Diller Frances Naylor	Aira Nordstrom Liz Phipps Marian Wattenbarger
Typists:	Evelyn Armstrong Carold Brady Renee Brignola Sharon Grantges	Ceil Langa Patricia Moran Linda Lott Rizzo
Special Assignments:	Janet Cavanaugh: Co-ordinator, July 15 through October 5, 1977 Elsalyn Drucker: Consultant on sources Linda Ellis: Newspaper account, Part III Mary Jane Finnerty: Correspondent	

ACKNOWLEDGMENTS

The AAUW Committee expresses its sincere appreciation to the following individuals and establishments for their contributions to the project: Nancy Adams, the E. A. Armstrong Agency of Little Silver, Alfred Aschettino, Thomas H. Auch, Lorraine Ayres, Elisabeth Thompson Babcock, Martin M. Barger, Philip C. Carling, Christ Church Middletown, Christ Church Shrewsbury, Christian Brothers Academy, Marvin A. Clark, Bart Coma, Major General W. Preston Corderman, Nancy Fatone, William Freedman (Eastern Branch Monmouth County Library), Dr. John Gallagher, Richard F. Grantges, Anita Hansen, Alan Holsey, Eleanor Holsey, Louise Jost, Claire Leonard, Robert W. Leonard, Joan Longo, Mrs. Marshall Lilly, Barbara Maryanski, Regina Mason, Vincent Miller, Linda Moran, Matthew Mullin, Jr., Elinor Multer, Rose Petraney, Edith Reilly, Margaret Schusterman, Dr. Donald H. Smith, Janice Speciale, Gershom Tomlinson, Leon Zuckerman, and the many other individuals whose interviews, letters, and other materials or services were important to the completion of this history.

"We've got to use the past to help the future."
—*Geraldine Livingston Thompson*

PART I:
A TRIANGLE OF LAND

Section I:
Beginnings by Dianne Petruzella

At 74° 10′ longitude and 40° 20′ latitude in Monmouth County, New Jersey, lies a triangle of land. It is bordered by Route 34 on the west and Route 520 (Newman Springs Road) on the north. Phalanx Road forms the triangle's southern boundary.

1. The Brookdale Triangle

Within the triangle lies an open and rural expanse made fertile by Hopp Brook, Big Brook, and an abundance of streams and ponds whose waters unite to form the Swimming River. The river runs northwest to southeast and forms a reservoir on either side of Phalanx Road.

On the upward slope of the reservoir's northeast shore sprawls a complex of brick, stone, glass, and weathered panelling—buildings at home on the landscape. White letters embossed on dark planks point the way to Human Affairs, the Gymnasium, the College Commons, and Forums 3, 4 and 5. Lights on tall poles punctuate the split rail fences. Walkways lead to white, barn-like buildings. This is the campus of Brookdale Community College, in Lincroft, New Jersey, occupying 221 of the more than 800 acres in the Brookdale triangle.

Brookdale Community College serves the whole community of Monmouth County. Its curriculum and extracurricular programs are responsive to the needs of county residents. The college reflects Monmouth County today. Yet what the college is today is an outgrowth of what has gone before: the lives of the earlier inhabitants of the land, and the events passing there.

The fertile land within the Brookdale triangle has been highly prized by those who have laid claim to it through the years. The farms of the early colonists flourished on this land. David Withers found its blue grass ideal for the raising of thoroughbreds. Geraldine Thompson, who loved nature and respected all of its creatures, viewed the land as a precious and irreplaceable resource. This same appreciation of the land and its beauty is reflected in the work of the college architects, who blended college structures into a whole with the landscape and used glass to bring the outdoors in.

2. The First People

The harmony of the college complex is the culmination of a tradition begun by the area's earliest inhabitants, the Raritan tribe of the Lenni Lenape Indians, who migrated from the West in search of a natural paradise. Their journey ended in Monmouth County; they were the first to inhabit and to treasure the land which is now the Brookdale campus.

The Lenni Lenape claimed that theirs was an ancient nation, originally located in a far-away country near salt water. They said that they left their home and traveled toward the land of the rising sun in search of "a red man's paradise" of deer and salmon and beaver. After many years of famine and fatigue, they came to "this beautiful country, where the ocean tides forever ebbed and flowed like the waters from whose shores they had come."[1]

They established their villages in the woodlands to the north, away from the ocean, where they could hunt and store their food during the winter. In summer, they migrated south to fish, establishing temporary villages.[2] In their travels, they followed the rivers or trails like the Minisink, or Burlington Path (now Sycamore Avenue in Shrewsbury).

For hundreds of years, the Indians of Monmouth County enjoyed a tranquil and solitary existence. That solitude was interrupted in September of 1609 when Henry Hudson's *Half Moon* anchored off the Navesink highlands.[3] The first meeting of Indian and white man was brief and somewhat fearful, but amiable. However, fear and suspicion grew until a few days later an Indian's arrow killed one of Hudson's scouts. Almost immediately, the *Half Moon* and its crew left the area. The Indians were not to be disturbed again except by an occasional trader until 1663, when English settlers came to purchase land.

During the years of settlement in Monmouth County, the English always purchased their land rights from the Indians, whom they respected and with whom they lived peaceably. In 1758, the colonial legislature purchased 3,044 acres (in what is now Burlington County) for the exclusive use of the Indians. This first American Indian reservation was called Edgepelick, then Brotherton, and finally Indian Mills. The

Indians later sold the land and moved to Oneida Lake, New York. They subsequently traveled to Green Bay, Wisconsin, and eventually to the Far West, the land of their origin.[4]

After the Revolution, the New Jersey legislature responded sympathetically to a request by an Indian warrior, Wilted Grass, who had fought along with the white men to free the colonies from British domination. When Wilted Grass maintained that the Lenni Lenape had never been paid for their hunting and fishing rights, the legislature appropriated $2,000 to pay the debt.[5] New Jersey's reputation for dealing fairly with the Indians remained untarnished.

From the beginning of the colonial period, the land on which Brookdale rests was the subject of dispute. It quickly developed political as well as natural value. Both English and Dutch laid claim to the area. The Dutch surrendered New York and New Jersey to the English in 1664, and although they regained title for a brief period they yielded permanently to the English ten years later.

3.
Early Claims
to the Land

For their part, the English could not agree on who was to rule New Jersey. In the late 1660's, both Richard Nicholls and Philip Carteret claimed the right to be governor. This rivalry for power—concluded only with the establishment in 1702 of a government controlled by Queen Anne—began the political dissension which continued throughout the colonial era.

While politicians were vying for control of the colonial government, Monmouth County was becoming a haven for refugees from other early settlements. Englishmen from Long Island purchased three "necks" of land from the Indians, and had their rights to the land confirmed by the Monmouth Patent, issued on April 8, 1665. The original patentees were Captain John Bowne, William Reape, John Tilton, Richard Gibbons, Samuel Spicer, Richard Stout, James Grover, William Goulding, Walter Clark, Nicholas Davis, Obadiah Holmes, and Nathaniel Sylvester (see Appendix I). Under the patent, these men became the owners of land encompassing the present Middlesex and Ocean Counties, and all of what is now Monmouth County, with the exception of Upper Freehold and the western part of Millstone Township.

The patentees were to parcel and develop the land as they saw fit. They were to make their own laws and try in their own courts all but criminal cases and civil cases involving sums over ten pounds. They were to pay no "rents, customs, excise, tax, or levy whatsoever"[1] for seven years, after which time they would be subject to the same taxes as others in the English territories. They were to have "free liberty of conscience, without any molestation or disturbance whatsoever in their way of worship."[2] Under the terms of the grant, the twelve patentees were required to attract the settlement of one hundred families within three years of April 8, 1665.

From 1665 to the early 1700's, small sailing vessels made frequent trips to Monmouth County, bringing settlers from Long Island and Rhode Island. The usual route was

... by sloop across the bay to the Wakake Landing, then by road to Middletown, from which place the usual way to Shrewsbury was by the road leading through Balm [Bamm] Hollow . . . to Ogden's Corner, by the John Bowne-Crawford ford, then through Morrisville . . . then, turning easterly, over through or near the present bridge on Leedsville road, and then the general course of the present road to Tinton Falls, and thence to Shrewsbury.[3]

This route followed old Indian paths which avoided steep hills, ravines, swamps, and deep streams. It is said that before there was a bridge on Leedsville (Lincroft) road, a traveler who attempted to cross the river found he had to swim his horse to reach the other side—hence the name Swimming River.

Although the initial settlements were established by those seeking religious freedom, others came to Monmouth County for economic reasons. One of these was Colonel Lewis Morris, a Welshman who had been sent by Cromwell to the West Indies to protect English interests there. When his brother's death brought Morris to New York in 1673, he heard about James Grover's profitable iron works at "the Falls at Shrewsbury." Morris persuaded Grover to sell him 3,540 acres including the iron works, and erected a house there, naming it Tintern Manor after his family's former home in Monmouthshire, Wales. (The name "Tintern" was later corrupted to "Tinton.")

Under Colonel Morris, the iron works was immensely profitable and of great benefit to New Jersey's economy. It required skilled workmen and employed a large number of both Negroes and whites in the mining of "bog ore." From 1676 to 1683 it furnished much of the material for iron works in Massachusetts and Pennsylvania.[4] Colonel Morris was also active in county government, and was responsible for naming the county Monmouth, after his native Monmouthshire.

William Leeds, Sr., was another Englishman who came to the county to improve his financial position. Leeds was a cooper, and he had hoped to make a good profit from his trade in the new colony. However, he recognized the potential of the choice farm land located in what is now Lincroft, and purchased acreage there from Richard Stout in February, 1679.[5] The property was in the southern part of Middletown, a short distance from Swimming River. Leeds purchased additional land from the Indians in 1680 and again in 1684.[6] He eventually accumulated 438 acres and it seemed that he would be a successful farmer.

For reasons which are not fully known, Leeds became disenchanted with his life in East New Jersey, and in 1690 he deserted his farm and his family. He left the property to his brother Daniel in trust for his son, William Leeds, Jr.

After 1682, Scottish immigrants began to land on Monmouth County's shores. These settlers were Quakers and Presbyterians, who, like so many before them, came to escape religious persecution in their homeland.

Among the first and most prominent Scots to arrive in Monmouth County was George Keith, from Aberdeen. Keith, an excellent surveyor, was commissioned as Surveyor-General of East New Jersey in 1684. Between 1685 and 1688 Keith surveyed and ran the line between East and West New Jersey.

His line was never fully agreed upon by the proprietors, but it still marks the western boundaries of Somerset and Monmouth Counties.[7]

Keith had been a Presbyterian in his youth, but later converted to Quakerism. In 1689, he left Monmouth County to become a Quaker preacher in Philadelphia. He was forced to abandon the faith, however, when he was publicly denounced for being "overbearing and aggressive."[8] Keith returned to England, converted to Anglicanism, and was ordained as a missionary. In 1702, he came to Monmouth County once again, and was responsible for converting many Quakers to Anglicanism.

Scots continued to flow into New Jersey, landing at Perth Amboy and dispersing through the nearby counties. The northwest border of Monmouth County was first settled by Scottish Presbyterians.

Several years after the Scottish influx, a group of Dutch came to the county. For the most part, they were the children of the Dutch in New York and Long Island. A peaceful and industrious lot, they moved to the area to avoid the overcrowded conditions of the original Dutch settlements. Between 1690 and 1720, the Dutch established prosperous farms and enjoyed a contented existence.

In contrast, the Scottish and English settlers shared an intense mutual dislike. The conflicts between the two contributed to the atmosphere of restlessness and rebellion which grew in the region during the late seventeenth and early eighteenth centuries.

4.
Keeping the
Faith

In an area founded by settlers in search of religious freedom, it is hardly surprising that the earliest social institutions were church congregations. And although the county had been officially divided into townships in 1693,* religious divisions had greater impact on the area's development than did geographical ones.

*Monmouth County was divided by the proprietors into three townships: Middletown, Shrewsbury, and Freehold. Boundaries were generally drawn to correspond with lines already found on the face of the landscape—rivers, streams, and old Indian trails.[1]

Prior to 1700, the major religious groups were Baptists (English), Presbyterians (Scots), and Quakers (both English and Scots). The Middletown Baptist Church was organized in 1668 and was allied with another church at Baptisttown, which later became Holmdel. The Presbyterians organized congregations in Shrewsbury and Middletown. The Quakers built their Meeting House in Shrewsbury in 1673. In 1702, however, the land ceased to belong to the "free-thinking" proprietors and became an English royal province. Enter: the Anglican Church.

Three figures who had much to do with establishing the Anglican Church in the county were the Reverend George Keith, the surveyor-turned-missionary; Lewis Morris, nephew of the Lewis Morris who had purchased the iron works in "the Falls at Shrewsbury"; and William Leeds, Jr., who had been left by his father to care for the family and tend the land in Leedsville.

The Reverend George Keith was the first missionary commissioned by the Society for the Propagation of the Gospel in Foreign Parts, an arm of the Anglican Church. He had the distinction of offering the first celebration of communion among those recently baptized into the Anglican faith. The service was held on Christmas Day, 1702, and both Christ Church in Shrewsbury and Christ Church in Middletown date their founding from that occasion.[2] (It was Christ Church, Middletown, which was to play such an important role in the life of Geraldine Thompson two centuries later.)

That first communion celebration was held at Tintern Manor, the home of Lewis Morris. It may fairly be said that the motives for Morris' religious activity were less than pure. He was a politician—he was appointed a judge at age twenty-one—and had his eye on the main chance. If the power were with England, then being influential in the Anglican Church in New Jersey was an avenue to power. Morris succeeded; he became Governor in 1738.

One church building erected in that period was Christ Church in Shrewsbury, which had as a vestryman

William Leeds, Jr. Leeds was one of the converts present at the first communion service at Tintern Manor. Although he is alleged to have had a youthful fling in the company of Captain Kidd when Kidd sailed Sandy Hook Bay, Leeds later became a devout churchman. On his death in 1739, he bequeathed his houses and lands to the Society for the Propagation of the Gospel for the benefit of congregations in Middletown and Shrewsbury. This Leeds tract became known as the Church Farm and later was part of Brookdale Farm. The property was nearly 438 acres on the Swimming River in Leedsville.[3] Leeds's body was interred near his house, but the grave was later moved to the cemetery at Christ Church, Shrewsbury.

The Church of England became part of the life of Monmouth County, but Anglicans were considered outsiders. In 1720, the Quakers, Baptists, and Presbyterians constituted the principal denominations and all were hostile to Anglican missionaries sent from England by the Society. Nevertheless, the Church continued to grow in strength and "in a colony where religious persecution . . . was illegal, Anglicans were tolerated."[4]

Anglicanism represented English authority, and as the eighteenth century progressed hostility toward English rule increased. Although religion had no part in the British ministerial policy, religious tensions became inseparable from the political conflict between England and its colonies.

5.
*Revolution
and Division*

Tolerance between dissenters and Anglicans came to an end with the outbreak of war; religious differences were transmuted into political ones. Because the Church of England had found fertile ground in Monmouth County, the area became a haven for those opposed to revolution. The patriots in the county were found among the Baptists, Presbyterians, and Dutch Reformed. The Quakers were pacifists, and remained neutral.

British ships appeared in Sandy Hook Bay in the spring of 1776. The appearance of the British intensified the activity of the Loyalists, most of whom belonged to the "New Jersey

Royal Volunteers," or "Skinner's Greens," named for their commander and the color of their uniforms. Many of these were honorable men who had been influential citizens of the province. They did not engage in plundering property, nor cause physical harm to the patriots, their former friends. However, other Loyalists, termed "Refugees," raised havoc in New Jersey, especially in Monmouth County. Any patriot, former friend or not, became prey to the marauding Refugees. They camped on Staten Island and at Refugees Town on Sandy Hook, where they were protected by the British fleet. From these bases of operation they mounted a campaign of continual harassment against Monmouth County citizens.

County residents fell victim not only to the Refugees but to the "Pine Robbers," named for the woods in which they hid. These "Pine Woods Robbers of Monmouth" were "the worst villains and desperadoes of the whole county."[1] They plundered and murdered for profit, terrorizing patriot and Tory alike. They were careful, however, not to incur the displeasure of the British, who reimbursed them for their booty.

While Monmouth County suffered the ravages of the Refugees and Pine Robbers, the British army moved in, taking much of New Jersey during the fall and winter of 1776. However, Washington's victories at Trenton and Princeton in December, 1776, caused a radical change. Deserters rejoined the army and many patriots-turned-Loyalist again allied themselves with the patriotic cause.[2] There were no further battles with the British in 1777, but the county was still subjected to raids by British troops and Refugees from Staten Island.

In May, 1778, the British ordered General Clinton to abandon Philadelphia and conduct his troops to New York. Clinton's march was to take him straight through Monmouth County to Sandy Hook. Washington's army, however, was in pursuit, and the Battle of Monmouth was engaged on June 28, 1778, in Freehold. Generals Lee, Washington, and "Mad" Anthony Wayne led the attack. With the arrival of dawn on June 29, it was discovered that the British had withdrawn to "the heights of Middletown." They then retreated to New

York. Although the Battle of Monmouth was not decisive, its conclusion was considered an American victory.

Throughout the war, New Jersey, because of its location, suffered more than other colonies. Of all New Jersey counties, Monmouth suffered most. Armies trampled the countryside and the Refugees and Pine Robbers deprived the people of their property and often their lives. Additional suffering was caused by the division of families and friends from one another as they were forced to commit themselves to either the Loyalist or patriot cause.

Religious worship was totally disrupted. Churches were destroyed, ministers killed, and congregations scattered. The Anglicans endured the greatest affliction. Many who had been British sympathizers and members of the Church of England fled at the war's end to Nova Scotia and the Bahamas.[3] Those who remained were branded as Tories, suffering recriminations and hostility. The wounds of war were severe, especially in Monmouth County.

6.
*Community
and
Prosperity*

Perhaps the strong religious faith that had prevailed in the county from the time of its first settlers contributed to peacetime development, even as it had been a contributing factor in wartime strife. The county began to prosper. Farms flourished, tourism developed, and the English sport of kings became the pastime of Monmouth County gentlemen.

The "greensand marl," discovered in the soil near Freehold and Middletown in the late 1700's, proved a great benefit to farmers. Where this natural fertilizer was spread, crops responded. By 1840, Monmouth farms were "under the highest state of cultivation."[1]

Vacationers and residents alike were enthusiastic about horse racing. Magnificent horses had been bred in the county since 1730, when a man named Gist had imported the notable Bubble Rock from England.[2] The bluegrass and the mild climate provided ideal conditions for grazing and breeding, and the county supplied many of the horses to Washington's army during the war years. As New York and New Jersey grew, horses were needed in even greater numbers—for transportation, for clearing land, and for pulling plows. Monmouth County farms furnished the horses. In Leedsville, Middletown, Holmdel, and Colts Neck, flatland was converted to private racetracks and racing became the premier sport.

Conditions in other parts of the nation were not so harmonious as they were in Monmouth County. The conflicting forces which led to the Civil War were gathering strength. In the Civil War as in the Revolutionary War, New Jerseyites were divided in their loyalties. Those who embraced the Union cause were highly visible in their support. The "Peace Democrats" and "Copperheads," however, were enraged by the Emancipation Proclamation. The *Monmouth Democrat* of Freehold, a rabidly anti-Lincoln newspaper, joined the protest.[3] Even the New Jersey Legislature passed "Peace Resolutions," in which they asked to have New Jersey men withdrawn from the Union Army and in which they listed numerous protests against Lincoln's administration.

The Peace Democrats and the legislature notwithstanding, the state of New Jersey gave a good account of itself in the Union cause.

The end of the war saw the burgeoning of the railroad industry. Both Monmouth County farmers and land developers were quick to see its potential. Trains carried crops to their markets and vacationers to their resorts. By the late 1860's New Jersey was home to the Jamesburg Railroad, the Raritan and Delaware Bay Railroad, and the New York and Long Branch Railroad.

The rail lines, as expected, proved a boon to an already prosperous economy. Summer resorts sprang up in the same areas enjoyed by Indian "vacationers" hundred of years before. Long Branch boomed. It was frequented by Presidents and became a playground for celebrities and gamblers, whose favorite diversion was horse racing.

Monmouth Park racetrack lured the Long Branch crowd. In 1879, the track was purchased by a group whose investment became very profitable. The racing season was increased from four days, in 1878, to twenty-five days, in 1888. Purses jumped from $12,600 to $210,850.[4]

The organizer of these successful Monmouth Park investors was David Dunham Withers, whose horse farm supplied the park with magnificent thoroughbreds. Withers' farm encompassed more than 800 acres; its land was fed by streams and brooks which joined to form the Swimming River. Withers named the farm Brookdale.

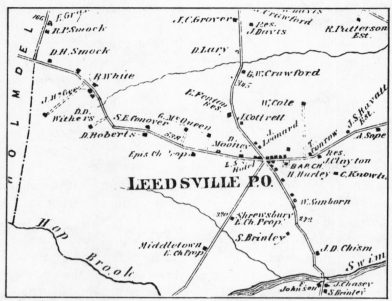

Atlas of Monmouth County, 1873: Portion showing Leedsville (Lincroft)

PART I:
A TRIANGLE OF LAND

Section II:
The Birth of Brookdale Farm by Linda Pollack

In a series of purchases ranging from 1872 to 1888, David Dunham Withers became the owner of over 800 adjoining acres (later known as the Brookdale triangle) in what is now Lincroft, New Jersey. Withers named his property the Brookdale Breeding and Stock Farm—also called simply Brookdale Farm—which became famous for the many fine race horses bred and trained there by Withers. Many of those who sold land to Withers had roots deep in Monmouth County's past and had made significant contributions to their communities (see Appendix II). His purchases included:

The Taylor Parcel: Michael and Sarah Taylor were the owners of the first parcel purchased by David Withers. In 1872 the Taylors sold to Withers 200.56 acres described as "a farm on the Holmdel to Red Bank Road." The price was $36,500.[1] The Taylors had purchased the land from Joseph Conover and his wife in 1869.

The McGee Parcel: The second parcel acquired by Withers was purchased in 1876 from Jerome and Catherine McGee. It included 123 acres on the Holmdel to Red Bank Road; the purchase price was $18,000.[2] The McGees had obtained the land from a sheriff's sale and from William S. Conover and Rulief Smock, assignees of Peter Smock.

The Smock Parcel: In 1879 Rulief (or Ruloffe) and Harriet Smock sold 78.21 acres plus .73 acres plus 1.01 acres to David Withers for a total sum of $12,500. The land was situated on "the road to Leedsville from Holmdel . . . along the line of John R. Smock."[3] The 1.01 acre portion was deeded by John's father, Peter R. Smock, in 1852, but the deed contains no recital of the origins of the other two sections.

The Leonard Parcel: Sarah Leonard, Mary E. Allen, Emma Sherman, George Sherman, William Leonard, and Ella S. Leonard sold a fourth parcel to David Withers in 1886. Withers paid $14,500 for 234 acres bounded on the north by the road from Leedsville to Holmdel, on the east by the "Church Farm," on the south by the Church Farm and the North American Phalanx property (see Appendix III), and on the west by Joseph Conover's property.[4]

The Oliver Parcel; the North American Phalanx: Also in

1886, Richard and Jane C. Oliver sold to Withers .32 acres and 10.49 acres consisting of "land in Atlantic Township, part of the land of the North American Phalanx."[5] This property had been conveyed previously to one Thomas Newbold by the North American Phalanx, and was conveyed in 1881 by William B. Newbold and Chilla Bosworth (heirs of Thomas Newbold) to the Olivers.

The Church Farm Parcel: David Withers completed his Brookdale tract with a purchase of 187.73 acres (plus a salt meadow of 2 acres) from the ministers, church wardens, and vestry of Christ Church, Middletown, Inc. This land, now known as the Church Farm section, was purchased for $12,671.77. It was described as on "the road to Leedsville . . .southwest corner Cyrenius Thompson yard down road to Phalanx. . . ."[6] The property had been conveyed by a partition deed in 1854 at the time of the separation of Christ Church into the Middletown and Shrewsbury churches.

This parcel is particularly interesting because of its history and the history of its former owners. *It has long been believed that this property, willed by William Leeds, Jr. to the church, became the site of Brookdale Community College. However, research shows that this particular parcel is now the property of the Lincroft School.*[7]

Withers' purchase of the Church Farm brought Brookdale Farm to a total area of 838.05 acres, land which cost him approximately $100,000 to acquire. Withers died less than five years after purchasing the Church Farm property. The tract was then sold in its entirety to another racing enthusiast, who was proud to carry on the Brookdale tradition.

I t's an ill wind that blows nobody good; it was the Civil War which brought horse racing to Monmouth County and to the triangle of land that became known as Brookdale Farm.

Racing had been suspended in the South, and many racing stable owners moved north, bringing their horses to safety. In response to the demand for racing facilities in the North, Jerome Park was built in 1866 just outside New York City. One of Jerome's fifty "life members," who held the power of

2.
"The Sage
of
Brookdale"

legislation over the track, was David Dunham Withers. He was a "leading spirit in 'the revival of racing.'"[1]

Although Withers was born in 1822 in New York, he spent his early adulthood in the South, where he owned cotton plantations and served as a member of the Louisiana legislature. He spent most of the Civil War years in France and England and became fascinated with European horse racing. When he returned to the United States, Withers sold his southern properties and joined his father, Reuben, in the East River Ferry Company in New York.

David Withers soon became president of the company and also was a director of the Bank of the State of New York. He was a large investor in the New York Ferry Company and during his lifetime he made a fortune from his ventures. At the time of his death he was thought to be worth between two and four million dollars.[2]

Withers' early interest in racing was further stimulated by his family's acquaintance with August Belmont, who came to New York from Virginia. Reuben Withers had assisted the racing magnate in establishing himself in the New York business community, and the Withers and Belmont families became close friends.[3]

During the revival of racing at Jerome Park, a racetrack was being built in Monmouth County. On September 13, 1869, J. McB. Davison and J. F. Chamberlain purchased 128 acres of land with a dwelling house, barn, and wagon house from one Richard R. Hullet. The price was $32,500.[4] This property was about a mile east of Eatontown and three miles west of Long Branch, near Little Silver, and had been part of the Corlies estate. Davison and Chamberlain fenced in the grounds and laid out a one-mile circuit racetrack.

The property was developed by the Long Branch and Sea-Shore Improvement Company, which issued stock to develop the tract and to build sheds, out-buildings, stables, grandstands, and a club-house. The company's principals were Charles G. Lloyd, Charles Height, Henry S. Little, Samuel Laird, and Francis Corlies. When the company went out of business, the property was foreclosed and sold to David Withers for $57,146.46.[5]

The title to the property was then conveyed to the Monmouth Park Association, which filed for incorporation in 1878. Withers was one of the organizers of the Association. In 1885, the capital stock of $60,000 was owned by August Belmont, David Withers, and Pierre Lorillard of New York; George Whitmore of Newport; and George Lorillard of Suffolk County, New York, who served as president of the Association.[6]

Improvements were made by the Association, and racing began in 1882. Space became inadequate and in 1890 a new, larger tract of 660 acres was purchased in Eatontown, on the site of what is now Fort Monmouth. The new Monmouth Park grandstand, which could seat 17,000 people, was at that time the largest ever built.

Racing, however, got off to a halting start. Following the first racing season in 1890, repressive legislation against gambling closed the track. After a reorganization in 1892, and just after Withers' death, the track re-opened for the 1892 and 1893 seasons. In 1894, gambling in general was prohibited by legislation. The racetrack was permanently closed, the land eventually sold, and the Monmouth Park Association dissolved. In time, public opinion changed and the present Monmouth Park opened on June 19, 1946, in Oceanport.

During his lifetime, Withers was known as "the Solon of the track" and "the sage of Brookdale." Sagaciousness was a quality much needed in those days, for until 1891 each racing association was its own governing body. Withers was not long in establishing a reputation for good judgment. According to Colonel N. Lewis Clark of Louisville, then the President of the Louisville Jockey Club,

No man in the country was more widely esteemed by racing men. He was perfectly square and honest. He was firm almost to obstinacy, and was emphatic in expressing himself, but he was firm because he believed he was right, and his judgment was respected.[7]

The growing popularity of racing led many to see a need for uniformity in the rules of racing, and on February 16, 1891, Pierre Lorillard formed the Board of Control. David Withers, representing Monmouth Park, was one of the seven members. This was the first step in general government in racing. Jockeys and trainers were licensed and the Rules of Racing were revised.

Tales of Withers' idiosyncracies abound. One of these was that he would bet nothing on his own horses. Although many others bet on the horses racing under Withers' color of black, Withers was most satisfied by the pride of victory and the winning stakes. His most successful year as an owner was 1889, when he started eleven two-year-olds, ten of which were winners. He netted about $70,000. In 1887 his horse, Laggard, won the Omnibus Stakes at Monmouth Park. In 1874 Withers had started the Withers Stakes, a race for three-year-olds, at Aqueduct Park, and won it himself in 1890 with his horse, King Eric.

Despite these victories, "a cruel fate seemed to follow this most deserving of owners."[8] Many of his horses developed physical problems which kept them from being winners. Withers was a good loser. "His forfeit, during the twenty years he raced, amounted to a fortune, yet his composure was such that even an occasional success could not disturb him."[9]

Because of his honesty and complete knowledge of racing, Withers often served as a judge in racing events. Once, at Monmouth Park, after a very unpopular decision which many were loudly denouncing, Withers stated: "The judges are in the stand to see how the race is run. They can see it better than anyone else. They did see it and their decision has been made. That settles it."[10] Withers would not be intimidated by the crowd and the decision stood.

The New York *Times* made note of Withers' ability to hold to a decision. In Withers' obituary, the *Times* said he

. . . had a keen intellect, a tenacious memory, and studied whatever he engaged in logically and in detail. He was an authority on racing matters.

He was vigorous, energetic, and decided in his opinions, and fearless in expressing them. As a result he made many enemies among the men with whom he associated.[11]

In addition to his important role at Monmouth Park, Withers also served as director of the American Jockey Club, and was a member of the New York and Coney Island Jockey Clubs. He was an honorary member of the French Jockey Club of Paris, and was one of the founders of the Knickerbocker Club.

Withers was fond of English horses but seemed to have more success with American stock. He cared a great deal for the care and comfort of his horses, and personally supervised the planning and construction of the buildings at Brookdale Farm. He ordered pine for the barns from North Carolina, and he, himself, drew the plans for the barns and stables, some of which stand today. The farm contained a training track and was noted for its beautiful, tree-lined pastures.

Withers used Brookdale as a weekend and summer home. The Brevoort House in New York City was his principal residence for more than thirty years, and he died there on February 18, 1892, after a brief illness. A bachelor, he was survived by three sisters and one brother. Because none of his relatives was interested in racing, Withers' beloved Brookdale Farm was sold to William P. Thompson in 1893 for $135,000.[12]

The land passed from one Thompson family member to another and at various times parcels were donated to others or sold. Today local residents recognize the original Brookdale Farm land as the sites for Middletown's Thompson Park, Monmouth County's Thompson Park, Lincroft Elementary School, Brookdale Community College, Monmouth Museum, and Marlu Farm. The 220.827 acre parcel which makes up the campus of Brookdale Community College was purchased for $700,000 in 1968 from the estate of Lewis S. Thompson, Jr.

PART II:
SEVENTY-FIVE YEARS ON BROOKDALE FARM

Section I:
The Thompson Era by Linda Lott Rizzo

Today, walking across the campus bluegrass, through the corncrib, and into the barns, one feels the aura of Brookdale Past. A sense of history pervades Thompson Park's mansion rooms and outbuildings where dynamic owners, faithful employees, active children, and superior horse breeding were part of an opulent era at Brookdale. Foot prints and hoofprints, impressed on the land, tell stories of its heritage.

Colonel William Payne Thompson was a horse breeding and horse racing enthusiast. A native of what is now West Virginia, he brought his family to Sea Bright, New Jersey, in the summer of 1891 (see Appendix IV). Two years later, Colonel Thompson purchased Brookdale Farm, which, until David Withers' death, had had the strongest stable in the East.[1]

When Colonel Thompson bought the farm from the estate of David D. Withers, the breeding and training facilities were already constructed and in full use. However, there was no main or manor house; Withers had lived in a small farmhouse during his visits to the farm. The mansion, now Thompson Park's Visitor Information Center, was built under Colonel William Thompson's direction. The Colonel kept about two hundred thoroughbred racing and breeding horses on the farm, including the prize horses One I Love (the two-year-old filly which won five consecutive races in 1895) and Requital (the 1895 Futurity winner).[2] Colonel Thompson's founding of the Monmouth Park Jockey Club was a valuable contribution to the sport of kings. When the Colonel died in 1896, he left the Brookdale property to his wife, Mary Evelyn, in trust for their three children—Lewis, Elizabeth, and William.

For a time, it seemed doubtful that Lewis Steenrod Thompson would live to inherit his share of Brookdale Farm. Like the woman who was to become his wife, he spent his young adulthood in a struggle against tuberculosis. It was life in the great outdoors which proved to be his salvation, and it was a life to which he was admirably suited.

Lewis Thompson was an avid sportsman. He won the International Pigeon Shot Championship at the tender age of nineteen, and later enjoyed living frugally with only "a tent, a horse, and a gun" in the Western wilds.[3] He is said to have held the unofficial title of "the finest shot of any man in the country."[4]

In January, 1896, Lewis Thompson paid a visit to his sister Elizabeth in Colorado Springs. Elizabeth had told him that she had found the woman he would marry. The woman in question was Geraldine Livingston Morgan, who was in Colorado recuperating from a bout with tuberculosis.

Elizabeth Thompson Preston proved to be an astute judge of character. Lewis and Geraldine were married at St. Margaret's Episcopal Church, Staatsburg-on-the-Hudson, New York, on June 16, 1896. Shortly afterward, Lewis and his bride joined his mother and brother William at Brookdale Farm.

**2.
Geraldine
Thompson:
Spirited
from the
Start**

Geraldine Thompson's forebears, the Morgans, Livingstons, and Hoyts, were as prominent in New York as were the Thompsons in West Virginia, New York, and New Jersey (see

A young and lovely Geraldine Livingston Thompson, approximately 1919.

Appendix V). When the new Mrs. Thompson came to Brookdale, she brought with her her family's long-standing commitment to public service.

In her dedication to the welfare of others, Geraldine Thompson reflected the drive and determination of her grandmother, Geraldine Livingston Hoyt, who had been active in the field of health services in New York. At one point in her philanthropic career, Mrs. Hoyt was rowed across the East River three times a week to visit the Blackwell (Roosevelt) Island Institution. There she took note of the living conditions of "New York's insane, murderers, the poor, and the sick, the afflicted, [and] the imbecile."[1] She told her granddaughters: "Hard work, courage, [and] patience make you change things."[2]

As a child, Geraldine Morgan displayed the same energy and fearlessness which were to become her trademarks in later life. The Morgan estate* in the upper Hudson region of New York State was six miles from Hyde Park, and Geraldine often played baseball with or against Franklin Roosevelt.[3] She was a good first baseman, and it is said that even as an adult she "knew the batting average for every professional baseball player in this country."[4]

In another, more dangerous game Geraldine and the local boys would dart single-file across the railroad tracks as the "Twentieth Century Limited" bore down upon them at eighty miles an hour. The last to cross was usually the youngest, the smallest, the instigator — Geraldine.[5]

The fun and games came to an end when Geraldine contracted tuberculosis in her young adulthood. It was the constant battle against illness that she remembered, looking back. Although the Morgans were not a wealthy family, "I was forced to spend my time traveling," she said. "I had tuberculosis."[6] Her own experience with physical suffering was undoubtedly a motivating factor in her concern for the physical and mental health of others.

---

*The estate in Staatsburg was expanded to 300 acres and is now Margaret Lewis Norrie State Park, named for Geraldine's older sister.

3.
Wife,
Mother,
Mistress
of
Brookdale

Geraldine Thompson's life expanded and flourished in three distinct areas: she became a wife, a mother, and the mistress of Brookdale Farm; she became involved in politics — specifically, the Republican Party; and she became a noted philanthropist and humanitarian.

The new Mrs. Lewis Thompson was a slender woman, five feet-four inches tall and a sharp contrast to her husband who towered over six feet. "She had the most amazing eyes," recalls her friend, Laura Harding, "and also a very strong chin." [1]

Young Mrs. Thompson entered her first role — that of wife, mother, and mistress of Brookdale Farm — quickly and efficiently. And efficiency was necessary; within a span of nine years, the mansion's rooms were to hold nine children. Soon after moving to Lincroft in the fall of 1896, Geraldine and Lewis Thompson traveled by train to Parkersburg, West Virginia, to bring a young orphan into their family. Anne Thompson, a twelve-year-old cousin of Lewis, had been orphaned at age two. Two separate sets of relatives who had served as guardians had also died, leaving her without a family and home. Anne returned with the Thompsons to live at Brookdale Farm. [2] The following year, on April 15, 1897, the first child of Geraldine and Lewis Thompson was born — William Payne Thompson III.

On December 7, 1899, Elizabeth Steenrod Thompson Preston, sister of Lewis, died shortly after the birth of her fourth child and third son. Her husband, Ralph Julius Preston, brought the four children, ranging in age from one week to five years, from Colorado Springs to Brookdale. The children, William, Jerome, Evelyn, and the baby, Lewis, were placed in the care of Geraldine and Lewis Thompson. [3] (Also in 1899, William Thompson, Lewis' younger brother, married and moved off the Farm and out of New Jersey, selling his share of the land to Lewis. The following year, Mrs. William Thompson, Sr., Lewis' mother, died.) [4]

And so it was that six youngsters were to live in the mansion before the Thompson's second child, Elisabeth [now Elisabeth Babcock], was born on September 27, 1900. The third Thompson child was Geraldine, nicknamed "Puss" and "Pussy," born on October 8, 1902. The fourth child, born on March 15, 1904, was Lewis Steenrod, named for his father and his grandfather's brother.

Ralph Preston moved his four children to New York City in 1907, but when the arrangement proved unsatisfactory, the children were returned to Brookdale Farm. At this time, a house was built on the portion of land which had been owned by Elizabeth Preston; the house became known later as the Preston House.[5] During the growing-up years of the Preston children, if one of them became ill he or she was sent to Mrs. Geraldine Thompson for nursing care. "Brookdale was the kindest house you could ever hope to find," asserts Elisabeth Thompson Babcock.[6]

The Thompson mansion was built by Colonel William Payne Thompson in 1893. He engaged the architectural firm of Carrerre and Hastings of New York, who designed and built within twelve months "the wooden Natchez-type Southern colonel, probably on the foundations, or part of the foundations of the farmhouse which [had] existed on that spot."[7] Although the mansion was partially destroyed by fire in 1910 and again in 1923, it was reconstructed both times on the original Carrerre and Hastings foundation. Either David D. Withers or Colonel William Thompson planted the trees surrounding the house. At one time, seventy-two giant elms grew in the vicinity of the mansion, but were killed by Dutch elm disease.[8] The Thompsons regretted losing their elms, and later in an article, "Mrs. Thompson Asks Goal for Humanity," appearing in the March 2, 1962, Asbury Park *Press*, Geraldine Thompson voiced her concern, suggesting that it would be "good to start a tree conservation program in the country."

The mansion is a three-story and basement structure, with twenty-nine rooms, thirteen fireplaces, and eleven bathrooms. A magnificent feature—one hidden from the public eye—is the two glass-enclosed cupolas, or turrets, on the roof of the mansion. One is reached by a staircase in the third floor bathroom closet, the other by a concealed staircase in a third-floor bedroom. The cupolas, built for Puss when she was convalescing from tuberculosis, are joined on the roof by a narrow catwalk.

When Geraldine Livingston Thompson moved into the Brookdale mansion in 1896, it was furnished in carved, heavy black oak. Over the years, as a result of fire or simply being discarded, the heavy furniture was replaced by many eighteenth-century English pieces. Mrs. Ella Kelly Stryker, a lifelong friend of the family, recalls that Mrs. Thompson's favorite color was red and that red carpets ran throughout the halls and up the staircases.[9] Other colors used in the house were gold, maroon, and blue.[10] Original paintings by Frederic Remington hung in the first-floor rooms.[11]

The paintings were overshadowed by Lewis Thompson's hunting trophies. "My father," recalls Elisabeth Babcock, was a world champion shot, [and] the hall (on the first floor) was entirely covered with open-jawed bear rugs, while the walls were well-covered with the heads of mountain lion and goats, elk, moose, deer and antelope. By gas light, the glass eyes on the wall and floor, the white teeth and scarlet jaws were enough to send small children flying upstairs.[12]

When the house bustled with children, Mrs. Thompson had a large domestic staff, including the children's governesses and nurses, a cook, a kitchen maid, two chambermaids, a housekeeper, a valet, a butler, and a parlor maid.[13] Mrs. Babcock notes that the children ate apart from the grown-ups and the ground floor was for the exclusive use of the adults.[14]

Geraldine Thompson entertained friends and guests in the sunny, paneled "butternut" room, her favorite, located to the left of the first-floor center hallway. Neither Mrs. Thompson, nor the Thompsons as a couple, entertained for the mere sake of entertaining; parties had a purpose and an objective that related to politics, social service, or children.

The mares with their foals, the paddocks of stallions, and the exercising of race horses were everyday sights at Brookdale Farm (see Appendix VI). In addition to its bluegrass pastures, the farm boasted several training tracks, including a mile-and-one-eighth track. Horses were part of the Brookdale Farm tradition.

4. Horses, Brookdale, and the Whitneys

In 1896, the Farm passed in ownership from Colonel William Payne Thompson to his wife, in trust for their three children. Lewis Steenrod Thompson and William Payne Thompson, Jr., continued to race under the Thompson colors of red and green. They employed James G. Rowe, Sr., to be in charge of the horse breeding and training at the Brookdale Stable, often referred to as the Church Farm. Under Rowe's supervision, Lewis and William won the 1897 Futurity with the filly L'Alouette.[1] The Thompson brothers' racing activities were disrupted that same year when

... the last hope of racing's devotees was destroyed by the adoption of a constitutional amendment (which passed by a mere three hundred votes) forbidding gambling in general and bookmaking in particular. At Monmouth Park, which was supported by as ethical and as devoted a group of turfmen as the country has ever known, racing was entirely abandoned.[2]

Among Lewis Thompson's personal friends were Harry Payne Whitney and Payne Whitney, sons of William C. Whitney. Harry Payne Whitney was a Phi Beta Kappa graduate of Yale who went into the mining business. He had a passion for horse racing. Under the colors of Eton blue and brown, H. P. Whitney "bred more good horses than any man in the history of the American turf—192 stakes winners."[3]

In the early 1900's, Harry Payne Whitney leased the Brookdale barns, pastures, paddocks, enclosed circular exercising track, half-mile tack, and mile-and-one-eighth track. The contract agreement was "for a $1 a year, with the understanding that Mr. [H. P.] Whitney would maintain them in top condition at his expense."[4] Mr. Whitney was obligated to pay the taxes and insurance on the above facilities, also.[5]

With the death of William C. Whitney in January, 1904, Harry Payne Whitney added to his breeding stock from his father's collection of horses. Although racing was suspended in 1911-1912, Whitney, among other horse owners, raced his abroad, primarily in England.[6] Horse racing resumed in New York in 1913 and Harry Payne Whitney's horses returned to the United States. Brookdale Farm continued to grow in reputation as a stud farm; indeed, "most turf-goers of the present have identified Brookdale with the Whitney name."[7] For over a quarter of a century, much of H. P. Whitney's success originated from Brookdale Farm.

James Rowe, Sr., was in charge of Brookdale's stud and training stables. Marshall Lilly, who started as an exercise boy in 1910, advanced rapidly to the position of assistant trainer, where his sense of timing and speed proved to be a great asset. The outstanding H. P. Whitney chestnut filly, Regret, was foaled at Brookdale and trained by Rowe and Lilly.

The filly "Regret" wins the Kentucky Derby in 1915.

The Whitneys' Greentree Stables, through Payne Whitney and his wife Helen Hay Whitney, purchased the Mullin, Conover, and McQueen farms and was relocated across Newman Springs Road from Brookdale Farm. Mrs. Payne Whitney developed steeplechase horses as well as race horses under the supervision of James Rowe and his son, Jimmy. The William C.-Payne Whitney Greentree Stables raced under the colors of watermelon pink and black.

The Thompson-Whitney financial arrangement covering horse expenditures at Brookdale Farm and Greentree Stables was unique. Wilfred Mullin (Brookdale Farm's accountant and later assistant trainer at Greentree) recalls:

In the 1920's, we had a revolving fund, just to show how much the Whitneys put into Brookdale. We had a bank account of $25,000. You'd pay the bills, the help, and what not. You'd send the statement to New York. . . . The [Payne] Whitneys in New York would send you back a check to cover the $25,000 you'd use each month. This was the monthly payroll.[8]

The barns on Brookdale Farm were moved from one place to another, and the new sites were often many acres and many miles away. A large barn on the present Christian Brothers Academy property provides an example: the barn stood originally on the Church Farm section of Brookdale. Matthew Mullin, Sr., manager of Brookdale Farm, Harry Payne Whitney, Payne Whitney, and James Rowe analyzed the annual needs of the horses and rearranged the barns and paddocks to meet those needs.

The contract and revolving $25,000 account continued from 1922 to 1932. Although in 1927 Harry Payne Whitney began moving his prime breeding stock to his new farm in Kentucky, his race horses continued to be trained and stabled at Brookdale Farm.[9]

After the death of H. P. Whitney, his son Cornelius Vanderbilt "Sonny" Whitney continued the horse training operations at Brookdale with Thomas Healey. At the same time, the Whitneys had an oval and training facilities for racing stock built on their 1,000-acre Kentucky breeding farm. When the Thompson-Whitney contract expired in 1932, Cornelius Whitney moved his remaining race horses to Kentucky. Brookdale's barns, paddocks, and training tracks were, for a time, deserted.

5. Child's Play Life for children on Brookdale Farm was rich and exciting. Employees' children played baseball with the Thompson children (see Appendix VII) and later with the Thompson grandchildren. The youngsters were taken to the beach at Sea Bright, and in later years swam in the swimming pool built on the front lawn of the Thompson mansion. The family's clay tennis courts were available for employees' use.

The children were given horseback riding lessons. Ella Kelly Stryker recalls her youth with Geraldine "Pussy" Thompson, daughter of Colonel* Lewis and Mrs. Thompson. "I remember lots of times two of us would be riding a horse.

*The honorary title of "Colonel" had been conferred on Lewis Thompson by Walter E. Edge, during the latter's term as Governor of New Jersey (1917-1919). The appellation remained throughout his life.

She used to take me for rides with her on the horse all
through the back woods and fields . . . it was just great as a
kid . . . they had ponies up there and all the children were
permitted to come up and ride the ponies." [1]

Children of local residents were welcome to play in the
fields, provided there was no property defacement or harm to
the animals, [2] and it was common for families to picnic on
Brookdale grounds. [3]

The health and well-being of all children was a prime concern of Mrs. Thompson, and this was reflected in the lives of
the Brookdale young people. One of the few rules set for
children, including Mrs. Thompson's own, was that no one
was to go near the stallion barns or paddocks. Elisabeth
Thompson Babcock remembers her early childhood on the
Farm:

> Little kids, such as we were 1904-1914, could travel the roads on
> the "Church Farm" on foot or on our ponies, and we could race our
> ponies on the half-mile track, we could scramble around in the woods,
> we could wade in the brook, but we could *not* go near the stallion barns
> unless we were with my mother, then no petting of the stallions. All
> Gold, a stallion which stood at Brookdale around 1919-1923, did all
> but kill a stableman. By 1915 we had more freedom. The stallion barns
> were still off limits but no other barns on the "Church Farm" area were.
>
> [Brookdale Community College's Administration Building] held the
> excellent hayloft over the stalls used for horses out of training due to
> illness or injury. I went out of the hayloft door thinking the rope was
> attached and landed with a thud some fifteen feet below. I doubt if
> there existed a tree worth climbing which I did not climb, but it was
> my mother who covered every inch of the pastures, fields, woods,
> banks, and lanes. [4]

Jim Walsh, an employee's child, recalls his parents' cau-
tioning him to avoid the woods and swamps.

> You could go anywhere you wanted to, but there was always the fear
> of getting lost . . . in the middle of the woods . . . in the summertime . . . .
> And you'd better have left yourself a marking, because you're not going
> to get out. . . . That happened to me on more than one occasion. [5]

46

The road between Broad St. and Shrewsbury Ave., Red Bank, approximately 1912.

Children received priority over material objects in Mrs. Thompson's value scheme. Barbara Niles, a tenant on the Farm, remembers vividly the afternoon that her son had a sudden fever of 105 degrees. It was customary to turn off the water to the tenants' houses every afternoon for a few hours, while the mile track and the alfalfa growing in its center were watered. When Mrs. Thompson learned about the sick Niles boy, she stopped the track watering and returned water power to the homes. Mrs. Niles was able to bathe her son and reduce his fever.[6]

Once, an employee's son severed his leg in a machinery accident. The accident was not related to Farm management or a result of Mrs. Thompson's negligence; nevertheless, Mrs. Thompson assumed the responsibility and paid thousands of dollars annually for many years, enabling the boy to have excellent surgeons, physical therapy, an artificial limb, and a secure future.[7]

Mrs. Thompson's love for children was reflected in the many parties she held at Brookdale to which her own children, employees' children, and children from the surrounding communities were invited. Wilfred Mullin remembers attending Christmas parties in the Thompson home when he was a child in the early 1900's. These annual Christmas parties were exciting occasions. A tree, at least twenty feet high with hundreds of lighted candles, stood in the first-floor hallway by the staircase. A man with a wet sponge on a stick watched the tree during the party. Mrs. Thompson gave each child a sweater or jacket, oranges, and candy.[8]

Later, during the forties and fifties, there were Thompson-sponsored Christmas parties held at the Lincroft church and Lincroft firehouse. Each year, local children and their parents participated in the Christmas pageant at the Church, then went to the firehouse for refreshments and gifts given by Santa.[9] Mrs. Thompson attended the Christmas festivities and enjoyed them as much as the children did.

Christmas was not the only holiday celebrated "in style" at Brookdale. Mrs. Helen O'Neill Grigor, an employee's daughter, reminisces about the Easter egg hunts she attended on the front lawn. "There were prizes given for the people that collected the most eggs."[10]

A child-oriented activity of Mrs. Thompson's that continues today is the annual pet show of The Monmouth County Organization for Social Service, which originated at Brookdale Farm. Today, the pet show is called the Frogtown Frolic and is held in Holmdel. Katherine Neuberger recalls one memorable pet show when Eleanor Roosevelt, a close friend of Mrs. Thompson, came up from Washington, D. C., to judge the pet categories and award prizes.[11]

Charles Harding recollects the year that penguins were a featured attraction:

... she had a man come from somewhere with a load of penguins. She had a swimming pool in front of the big house. . . . The penguins were playing around the pool all afternoon, and the man who had trained them to do all kinds of things and the kids were having a marvelous time. Finally, it came time for him to go home. So, he and his helper had a net that stretched across the pool with a pole on each end, and they herded the penguins all the way down to the end of the pool where they could catch them. But the penguins were too smart; they would dive under the water and wouldn't come up. So this went on for hours, and this intrigued everyone more than anything that could have happened.[12]

6. Educational Concerns

Education was of prime importance to both Colonel and Mrs. Thompson. They gave abundant time, energy, and money to many educational endeavors. "You know," stated Mrs. Thompson, "the only reason I can belong to the American Association of University Women is because Rutgers gave me an honorary degree of Doctor [sic] of Philanthropy" [in 1931].[1] Although this honorary degree was the first of many, Mrs. Thompson, in her later years, spoke with regret that she had not had a college education. Laura Harding recalls Mrs. Thompson's words: "One remark that she used to make to me was . . . how much more effective you could be if you had had a college education. The discipline of that would have made you more effective."[2]

Mrs. Thompson aided many students with college expenses and gave scholarships through many organizations. Countless anonymous gifts assured youngsters' educational opportunities.

The young employees at Brookdale Farm received instruction, too. Over seventy exercise boys boarded on Brookdale Farm and worked with Harry Payne Whitney's horses. The boys cared for the horses from daybreak until noon, had meals prepared by Whitney's staff and cook, received winter and summer sets of clothing, and were paid good wages. Traditionally exercise boys did not receive any formal education, but through Mrs. Thompson's insistence lessons were provided for them. Every afternoon, the boys attended classes in the weighing station at Brookdale, where Mrs. Lilly, first wife of Marshall Lilly, was their teacher.[3]

Colonel Lewis Thompson also was deeply interested in education and served on the Middletown Township Board of Education. At one time, he gave an athletic field to one of the Middletown schools.[4] He also provided transportation for all Lincroft-Everett students traveling to the Leonardo Schools (seventh and eighth grades and high school), in the twenties. A bus drove the pupils to and from Red Bank, where they took the trolley to Leonardo.[5]

The children of Brookdale employees attended the elementary school in Lincroft. Wilfred Mullin recalls the old, yellow schoolhouse on Newman Springs Road, located on the Lincroft side of the present Garden State Parkway. In 1908, a new red brick building was erected near the Lincroft Inn, opposite what is now the Lincroft Elementary School. "So then, we didn't have so far to walk [from Brookdale Farm]." Mr. Mullin remembers Colonel Thompson's having men "dig out the cellar underneath the school and put in a big furnace for the heating system. And also he piped the water from Brookdale pumping station down to the schoolhouse, so there would be running water at the schoolhouse."[6]

The elementary school in Lincroft.

Mrs. Thompson was instrumental in arranging the first school program for migrant workers and their children. The Migrant Farm Workers' School, held in Freehold, provided education, as well as clothing, food, and bus transportation for its students. Dr. Joseph E. Clayton, then Monmouth County Superintendent of Schools, shared Mrs. Thompson's concern for the needs of the seasonal workers.[7]

It is ironic that neither Colonel nor Mrs. Thompson, both of whom understood the importance of education, was to know that their land was destined to become the beautiful campus of Brookdale Community College. Elisabeth Thompson Babcock says of her mother:

She cared for education in the deepest sense. Had your college come in the middle of her life, I expect you might have had to appoint her an Honorary Professor of any number of subjects from baseball to climbing Mt. Everest, from prison reform to a battle cry for fairness, courage, and forgiveness."[8]

7.
Hither and
Yon:
Automobiles
and
Airplanes

The invention of the automobile altered the lives of the Thompsons and people in the Lincroft area. Mrs. Thompson used the automobile as a means of expediting the business of her many organizations; it enabled her to drive to the homes and offices of people with whom she was involved. One woman comments that when Mrs. Thompson wanted something, "she would often arrive at a very early hour, like about 7:30 in the morning . . . sit down and say what she wanted. And some people simply couldn't take it, and some people wouldn't take it, and some people were utterly fascinated. And she got what she wanted."[1]

When asked to categorize his mother's driving, Mrs. Thompson's son Lewis stated that she was "the kind of a driver that blows at railroad crossings."[2] An employee's son remembers when he was eight years old seeing Mrs. Thompson in her 1947 Lincoln "doing eighty M.P.H. . . . I can remember my uncle running off the road because 'Here she comes,' and being scared of her in a car because of that. Every time you heard Mrs. Thompson coming, you'd run for the bushes. But none of that was true! As a kid, you're very impressionable."[3]

In spite of the tales of her rapid driving, Mrs. Thompson was very aware of speed and its danger. To assure the safety of tots at Brookdale, she had "bumps" built in the main driveways. Cars and vans were forced to slow down to four m.p.h. in order to creep over the series of bumps.[4]

Although the automobile served Mrs. Thompson's purposes, she became annoyed with the heavy New York City traffic. On one occasion, she startled her chauffeur considerably. Upon reaching Mrs. Thompson's business destination, the chauffeur opened the back door for her to step out, but there was no passenger in the back seat. Somewhere in the bog of traffic, Mrs. Thompson had slipped out of the car and had walked the rest of the way to the building. In fact, she arrived there before her automobile.[5]

Colonel Thompson was among the first people in Monmouth County to have an automobile. He owned several, two of which were a Boule and a Renault racer.[6] The Thompsons understood the value of the automobile to progress. Jim Walsh reminisces, "Milton Brownlee was the first Chief of Police in Lincroft . . . and [they had] a car given to them by Mrs. Thompson, a 1937 Ford, four-door sedan, black, with a bubble on the top."[7]

The coming of the automobile had an irreversible impact on the tiny community of Lincroft. Wilfred Mullin states, "The construction of the Garden State Parkway has caused a tremendous change. . . . It opened it [Lincroft] up as a residential area . . . that's when development really started. It started right next to the Parkway and gradually came up through Lincroft."[8]

The airplane too had an impact on Brookdale. Colonel Lewis Thompson played an important dual role in aviation; he loaned Brookdale's facilities to the United States Government for the testing and repairing of airplanes in World War I, and he was instrumental in the mobilization of the First Yale Unit, a group of young men interested in learning the fundamentals of aviation.

Wilfred Mullin recalls airplanes landing and taking off at the north end of the large race track oval.[9] Camp Vail Signal Corps, later renamed Fort Monmouth, used the landing field. The government utilized Brookdale's machine shops, grinding tools, and lathes. Matthew Mullin, Jr., remembers ". . . airplane motors were tested and rebuilt and the planes themselves took off and landed on the forty-acre field."[10] Also on loan to the government during World War I was George Mauser, Mr. Thompson's "truly outstanding mechanic."[11]

Colonel Thompson's second contribution to aviation was the first Yale Unit. In 1916, the Colonel and a group of young Yale men gathered at West Palm Beach, Florida, to undertake the intensive aviation training course. The New York *Herald Tribune* reported:

Later, the unit moved north to Huntington, Long Island. Colonel Thompson went with the young men. Then came the war and the youthful flyers were enlisted by an eager Navy Department. The unit, equipment and all, was taken over by the government for the nominal sum of $1, although its value was thousands of times that sum.[12]

Those contributing money for the project were J. P. Morgan and Co., Henry P. Davison, G. P. Baker, Jr., Payne Whitney, Harry Payne Whitney, and Colonel Thompson.

8.
Family
Life

Children and the activities she shared with them were a major source of joy to Mrs. Thompson. Reading the Bible together was an intimate experience that both Mrs. Thompson and her children enjoyed and cherished. Each evening before the children went to bed, they gathered in their mother's bedroom to hear and watch the dramatization of Biblical figures and events, brought to life by Mrs. Thompson.[1]

Geraldine Thompson, like her mother and grandmother, shared news of her interests and projects with her children. Elisabeth Babcock recalls, "We couldn't wait until they [Mrs. Thompson, et al.] came home to hear who won the battles. . . . To us, it was like today's children listening [to] and watching exciting tales on television."[2]

Mrs. Babcock emphasizes her mother's love and concern for her family: "First came her family—her husband, mother, sisters, brother, and children. She would drop all other responsibilities to care for them. You could absolutely count on her rushing to the rescue and being with you until you were safe again or dead."[3]

Colonel Thompson's passion for hunting, fishing, and the outdoor life established a pattern for his family's activities. During the first few years of their marriage, Mrs. Thompson joined her husband for brief vacations in the Rocky Mountains. Mrs. Thompson was an expert marksman and could "shoot and hunt as well as a man."[4] The Thompson gun collection was considered one of the best in the state of New Jersey.[5]

The Colonel's transient life-style, however, did not mesh with that of Mrs. Thompson, whose responsibilities with home and children were increasing. Also, Mrs. Thompson was becoming a participant in local and state politics and social service activities. The divergent interests of the Colonel and his wife resulted in the following annual pattern: When the children were young, "the whole family was together for two months of the year at Upper St. Regis Lake in the Adirondacks where the Thompsons [rented] a summer camp."[6] Late in summer, the Colonel went fishing for salmon in Canada. (One Brookdale friend remembers receiving salmon shipped to the Farm in crates of ice.)[7]

In autumn, the children returned to boarding school or went with Mrs. Thompson to Brookdale Farm, and the Colonel enjoyed duck hunting at Long Point, Lake Erie, or at Montauk Point, Long Island.[8] In the 1920's, when the duck hunting season was shortened, he began traveling to Nova Scotia to open the season and then proceeded to "follow the ducks" down the coastline to Mexico for four months of uninterrupted duck hunting.[9]

From November to April, Colonel Thompson hunted quail, duck, and doves at Sunny Hill, a 12,500-acre plantation he had purchased in Thomasville, Georgia. He won trophies and ribbons in field trials with his prize hunting dogs.[10]

When the children were of school age, the Thompsons lived in New York City in the winter. Firewood, flowers, and vegetables from the Brookdale greenhouses went to the New York residence with Mrs. Thompson. Some of the Brookdale employees accompanied her. The Colonel usually stayed in New York briefly and with his wife visited museums and the opera; then he traveled South. For a month or two, Mrs. Thompson vacationed with her husband at their Georgia plantation, and throughout these cold months different family members visited the plantation when it was convenient for them.

In May, the Colonel went fishing off the Florida Keys. By

June, the cycle was completed and the whole family gathered together again at Brookdale Farm in preparation for the summer stay in the Adirondacks.

In his later years, Colonel Thompson became an expert wildlife photographer. Switching from gun to camera, he "shot" close-up action pictures of animals and birds. Also later in his life, he was active in the development of the bob-white quail. Mrs. Thompson shared her husband's concern for animal and bird research and conservation, and became an ardent supporter of the National Audubon Society.

In addition to activities shared with her husband, Mrs. Thompson cultivated her own hobbies. Jogging was an important part of her daily early morning routine, and she "was also proficient at tennis, winning a number of tournaments handily."[11] Mrs. Thompson believed swimming was a beneficial form of exercise; she had a swimming pool installed in her front lawn, to be used by herself, her children and grandchildren, and her employees.

Tuberculosis was a concern and first-hand experience for Colonel and Mrs. Thompson and, unfortunately, for their daughter, Geraldine. The Colonel's outdoor way of life appeared effective in combating his tuberculosis. For many years, he served as a member of the board of trustees of Trudeau Sanatorium, Trudeau (near Saranac Lake), New York,[12] the same institution where his daugther spent periods of time recuperating from tuberculosis attacks.[13]

Mrs. Thompson overcame tuberculosis as a young woman and continued a rigorous outdoor exercise and walking program for herself during her adult life. She was always aware of the dangers of the dread disease, showing compassion for anyone who showed its symptoms. The story is told that early one evening, a group of Harry Payne Whitney's exercise boys carried a critically ill friend to the Thompson front porch. Recognizing the symptoms of a TB crisis, Mrs. Thompson gave orders for a doctor to be summoned and for ice to be brought from the ice house and packed on the youth's chest. She cradled and rocked the boy in her arms until, hours later, he died; the next day, she arranged for all Whitney employees to have chest X-rays.[14]

The Thompsons' interest in the prevention and treatment of tuberculosis led to their initiating the legislation which resulted in the building of the "first (TB) preventorium in the country," Allenwood Sanatorium in Allenwood, New Jersey.[15] Also, before the establishment of Allenwood, Mrs. Thompson was known to have financed local people who had tuberculosis, sending them to Tucson, Arizona, or Saranac Lake tuberculosis centers.[16]

Geraldine "Puss" Thompson, age 18, in 1920.

Lewis Steenrod Thompson, Jr., age 12, in 1916.

Colonel Thompson's health began to decline in 1933. After a brief illness, he died on March 26, 1936, at his Sunny Hill Plantation in Georgia. His wife sat at his bedside during those last weeks, and although she concealed her grief no one doubted that his death was a sharp blow to her.

Diverse interests had separated the couple physically for months at a time, but they had remained together in spirit. Laura Harding remembers Mrs. Thompson's telling her "that . . . all her romantic kind of thrill was produced by the sight of the Colonel when they first met. And I think to her dying day, he still was this image of romantic, thrilling love. . . . It didn't matter [that they were not together that often]. The image stayed in her mind."[17]

Tragedy struck repeatedly at the seemingly impervious Geraldine Thompson; three of her children—William, Geraldine, and Lewis—predeceased her. In 1952, Mrs. Thompson had given the section of her property that would later become the site of Brookdale Community College to her only surviving son, Lewis S. Thompson, Jr. She hoped that some day he would return from Washington, D. C., to make his home at Brookdale and keep all that was left of Brookdale in the family.[18] Her wish was not to come true. Although Lewis stabled thoroughbred race and stud horses at Brookdale Farm under the supervision of trainer Thomas Harraway, he never relocated permanently at Brookdale Farm.

9.
The Village

Today's Lincroft Village, with its many housing developments, strings of stores, expansive public and parochial schools, and busy five-road intersection, is in sharp contrast to the Lincroft hamlet of seventy-five years ago.

In the early 1900's, the Lincroft "crossroads" had a small cluster of shops. The Lincroft Inn was a noted stagecoach stop on the "run" from Lakewood to New York. Willie Reed's saw mill, situated behind the Lincroft Inn, cut logs into the rails that became Brookdale Farm's black and white border fences. Locust trees were made into posts.[1] East of the crossroads, the north side of Newman Springs Road held large farms and the south was dotted with small vegetable (truck) farms.

An important spot at the crossroads was Johnny Conover's general store, one of the meeting places of the village. "They sold candy, kerosene, chicken feed, and everything else," recalls Matthew Mullin, Jr.[2] Behind the present-day Lincroft Elementary School was Bill Hurley's blacksmith shop, another important site in a community which held two grandiose horse farms. Freedy Langendorf operated Lincroft's first gas station near Coronet Street on Newman Springs Road.[3]

Westward on Newman Springs Road from the Lincroft Inn, the north side of the road contained a small group of homes

The Lincroft Post Office early in the century.

and the red brick school built in 1908. Next came the Whitney estate, Greentree Stables. Opposite Greentree was Brookdale Farm. The pond on the Brookdale side (located beyond the present Thompson Park entrance) was dug about 1911, under the direction of Matthew Mullin, Sr., to be a source of water in case of fire.[4]

There were many memorable figures in that early Lincroft Village community. Frank "Fibber" McGree, a farmer, "could make more money off poor land than most folks could with good land."[5] George Mauser, Brookdale's remarkable mechanic, "used to grow his own tobacco supply behind his house."[6] "There was Bill Van Brunt who worked at Brookdale, but got up at five a.m. to feed his own horses before reporting to the Thompson Farm."[7]

Even a partial listing of Brookdale's employees in that period conveys the magnitude of the Farm operation. There were, among others, Mr. Barney Kelly, Mr. Martin Kelly, Mr. James Vaughan, Mademoiselle Laure Bandelier, Miss Mary Kelly, Miss Madge Smith, Mr. [H. H.] Reynolds, Mrs. Flanagan, Mr. Harold Kelly, Mr. Matthew Mullin, Sr., his sons Wilfred Mullin and Matthew Mullin, Jr., and granddaughter Miss Martha Mullin, Mr. and Mrs. David (Pa and Ma) Hood,

Mr. James Rowe, Sr., and Mr. James Rowe, Jr., Mr. and Mrs. Marshall Lilly, Mr. Taylor, Mr. George Mauser, Mrs. B. Price, Mr. Gaffney, Mr. Woodstead, Mrs. Gray, Mrs. Pauline Harvey, Mr. O'Neill, Mr. Walsh, and Mr. Luther Schank. They attended to the personal, domestic, and business needs of the Thompsons; they were responsible for farming; they cared for the land and the buildings; they raised and tended the horses.

10.
Change

The removal of Cornelius Vanderbilt Whitney's horses, the 1932 termination of the Thompson-Whitney contract, and the death of Colonel Lewis Thompson created a financial re-evaluation of Brookdale Farm. The funding provisions in Colonel William Payne Thompson's will expired when his son, Colonel Lewis Thompson, died in 1936. "The wherewithal to carry it [Brookdale Farm] would have perished with my father,"[1] states his daughter Elisabeth Thompson Babcock.

From 1934 until Mrs. Thompson's death in 1967, the Brookdale barns were leased to independent trainers. A revolving fund contract, like the Thompson-Whitney contract, was never duplicated. The section of Brookdale Farm that later became Brookdale Community College was leased to one Mr. O'Leary until about 1940, when Thomas Harraway

A corner of Marlu Farm, once part of Brookdale Farm.

leased the facilities. He remained at Brookdale until after the property was sold to the Board of Chosen Freeholders in 1968. The barns located on the present Thompson Park section of Brookdale Farm were rented to local residents for boarding their horses, and to Monmouth Park Race Track during the summer racing season.[2]

In 1940 and 1941, Mrs. Thompson sold the western sector of Brookdale Farm, land that extended into Holmdel and had been used for livestock pastures, orchards, and grain and vegetable fields, to Mr. Maurice Pollak, who named his dairy farm property Marlu Farm. "I don't think she could have borne to sell an inch of Brookdale to anyone but Mr. Pollak," says Elisabeth Babcock.[3] "She liked him very much, had great respect for him, and knew that he intended to use the land for a dairy farm."[4]

When Monmouth County had an extreme housing shortage during World War II, Mrs. Thompson served the government by converting the vacant outbuildings into furnished living quarters for Fort Monmouth personnel and their families. "I started at one end of the farm and examined every building," she said. "Jockey quarters, barns, and dining rooms were altered wherever possible. Before we finished there were twenty-nine apartments . . . I even converted the third floor of my own home into an apartment."[5]

One of the notable renovations was the spacious, three-story, stucco Preston manor house; it was converted into six apartments. In 1953, Mrs. Thompson considered offering the Preston House and six acres of surrounding land to Monmouth Memorial Hospital as a rehabilitation center for polio patients.[6] (Mrs. Thompson's granddaugher Alice [Mrs. Stacy Lloyd], a polio victim, lived at Brookdale Farm in 1950, in order to take advantage of Monmouth Memorial's physical therapy department.) The plan, however, did not materialize. In 1961 fire destroyed a great portion of the six-apartment Preston House, and the remainder of the structure was demolished.

Housing facilities on Brookdale Farm continued to be rented until Geraldine Thompson's death in 1967. Stipulations in her will granted the tenants a year to relocate following her demise. Mrs. Thompson had had great respect for the tenants at Brookdale. "Our American families are the greatest and finest in the world," said Mrs. Thompson. "I know. I've learned it first hand."[7]

Those same adjectives, "great" and "fine," were also to be used many times in reference to Geraldine Thompson, a remarkable individual who brought great honor to the triangle of land that was Brookdale Farm.

PART II:
SEVENTY-FIVE YEARS ON BROOKDALE FARM

Section II:
The Great Lady of Brookdale by Meline Karakashian

1.
Profile:
Geraldine
Livingston
Thompson

Many knew Geraldine Livingston Thompson as "New Jersey's First Lady," "The Great Lady of Brookdale," "The First Lady of Monmouth County," or just as "Mrs. Thompson"; a select few had the privilege of calling her "Granny." Early in this century, when Monmouth County's and New Jersey's social services and health institutions were either primitive or nonexistent, this dynamic woman had the perception and humanitarian vision to work for reform of the existing institutions and to plant the seeds for social welfare organizations. She launched a great campaign to reach the needy, the disadvantaged, and the handicapped and to make their lives more enjoyable.

People who knew the colorful personality of Geraldine L. Thompson, her philosophy of "social engineering," and her life's accomplishments, do not find it surprising that a college like Brookdale—geared to serve the educational needs of this community and to encourage community involvement in various cultural, social, civic and political programs—came into existence in Monmouth County. The seeds that she had planted found a receptive environment in her beloved estate.

Mrs. Thompson's daughter, Elisabeth T. Babcock, describes her mother's daily routine:

... just the sight of a large old house and the picture of a domestic staff would seem to place "the lady of the house" in a gilded chair, her feet on a cushion, an ostrich feather on her head. She never changed her itinerary. She rose at six a.m., ran over to the mile-and-one-eighth track, ran around this, jogged home, took an ice cold bath, dressed, knelt and said her prayers, had breakfast, jumped in her car, and off she went to Trenton, to Vineland, to Jamesburg. . . .[1]

If she got home by one p.m. she would eat a spare lunch, then take a snooze. Then off again on foot with her dogs from one end of Brookdale to the other.[2]

"She could channel her physical resources better than anyone I ever knew,"[3] wrote Beatrice O. Freeman, a newspaper reporter who had known her for more than twenty years.

She astonished doctors with the mileage she got out of that frail body of hers. An eminent geriatrician who examined her in her mid-eighties warned that her heart was so bad, she had better take it easy.

"But her heart has been that bad for the last twenty years," her life-long family physician pointed out.

That summer Mrs. Thompson spent two weeks at the Audubon Camp on Hog Island off the coast of Maine [a yearly custom]. She tramped through the woods, swam in the icy Atlantic, took her turn waiting on tables, and played a seal in a camp play.

Some months later, she telephoned her daughter, Mrs. Elisabeth Babcock. "Betty, dear, something dreadful happened this morning."

"What is it Mamma?"

Mrs. Thompson, then eighty-five, admitted she had been jog-trotting around a mile-and-an-eighth horse training track at Brookdale Farm every morning before breakfast.

"But I couldn't make it this morning. I had to walk part of the way."

Nevertheless, at ninety she still bounced down stairs with the impetuosity of a teenager. On her 92nd birthday, I found her . . . on a bitterly cold day, ankle-deep in snow, feeding the ducks on a pond below her house. . . .[4]

Miss Freeman adds, "A few months before her 94th birthday, an elderly friend asked the secret of her youthfulness. 'Keep working for at least one cause, preferably an unpopular one,' she replied."[5]

2. An Unpopular Cause

Her "unpopular" cause was helping people. Former Senator Richard R. Stout comments: "She was very much like Mrs. Eleanor Roosevelt and the two were friends, as you know. They were interested in helping the handicapped and helping the unfortunate and disadvantaged."[1] Senator Alfred N. Beadleston adds, "Her principal goal in life was to help the lot of the unfortunate through charitable things. She was always out to help the underdog, the unfortunate, to help the sick and the poor. . . ."[2]

"I'm at the White House, what can I do for you?"[3] Geraldine L. Thompson's cheerful voice would occasionally sound on the telephone. She was always ready to be helpful to friends, neighbors, anybody who needed assistance. It is said that whenever anyone in the Lincroft community needed help, health care, or shelter, he would be referred to Mrs. Thompson. Her children, well aware of their mother's inclinations, would often seek her help for a neighbor. Mrs. Babcock remembers:

When I was eight and my sister six, we were told we could take our ponies off Brookdale and go riding around the countryside. So, feeling like Columbus, off we went bareback on our little, fat ponies. We went towards Middletown and then took the road to the left, which ends up on Everett. There was just an old house on that road, and it was on brick pilings that were crumbling and it had no front door. The front yard looked like the back yard—there were bits of bricks and old cans and long-legged, scrawny chickens, and the house desperately needed painting. There was a boy sitting on the side of the bank and he had on knickerbockers and a white shirt . . . a nice little face with freckles. He got up slowly, so as not to scare the ponies, and he said, "Could you please, please help me?"

So, we tied the ponies to some saplings and we crossed this yard and went to the back of the house and up these plank steps into the kitchen. There were two iron beds in the kitchen and in one was the father and the mother, who were too sick to raise their heads, and in the other bed was his older sister who was about sixteen years old and a baby brother who was about four, too sick to raise their heads. There was a sink with a pump and cold water; and there were cans and dirty dishes, and this poor kid, the only one who could stand up on his feet. He said, "Can you please, please help me?" We knew if we got Mamma, she could do it, so we said "yes." We scampered away and we kicked our fat ponies' stomachs and galloped them all the way to Brookdale and raced up the stairs and we said, "Mamma, Mamma, come and save these people." She was able to save the older sister and the little brother, but the nice boy who asked for our help and his mother and father all died of tuberculosis.

If my mother found one case, she was like a bird dog: how many more were there? Then [she] started the legislation to build the first tuberculosis hospital in the county [Allenwood].[4]

Katharine Elkus White met Geraldine Thompson when Mrs. Thompson asked her to serve on the board of Allenwood Tuberculosis Sanatorium. "Her interests were in doing good, really,"[5] sums up Mrs. White. Katherine Neuberger, who knew Mrs. Thompson well, agrees. "She believed in helping people," says Mrs. Neuberger.

She [especially] used to talk about the people ... who had small homes and were having a tough time making ends meet. She was very charitable to individuals, much more so than she was ... to organizations. And she, for instance, would pay for college education for people in the village (Lincroft) and she never wanted anyone to know that.[6]

Mrs. White also remembers Mrs. Thompson as "an ardent churchwoman."[1] Her daughter, Elisabeth, once wrote to a reporter that, "Her husband, all her children, her mother and sisters, all those on staff and the farm came just after her Divine Creator; then all the people of New Jersey, particularly the ill, the old, the young, and anyone in trouble."[2]

3. An Ardent Churchwoman

Mrs. Thompson taught at several Sunday Schools through the years: at Grace Episcopal Church in New York City; at All Saints Episcopal Church in Navesink; and during and after World War II at Christ Episcopal Church in Middletown, since it was closer to her home. Her memorial service was held at this last church. She is remembered by her friends as feeling perfectly at home in the church, on occasion sharing her thoughts about a sermon with an "Amen" or an "Oh, no," warming her feet on the grate where the heat came up during cold winter days.[3] Laura Harding, a lifelong friend, says, smiling, "The world was her home. She saw a great deal of the minister of the church ... [who] came over a lot, talked to her and prayed with her."[4]

Elisabeth
Thompson
Babcock
at age 18.

My mother's mind and heart had little or no time for furniture, furnishings and clothing,"[1] wrote Elisabeth Babcock to a reporter. And her friends tend to chuckle when they describe Geraldine Thompson's attire.

Although she was a wealthy woman who contributed large sums of money through the years to social service organizations, to political campaigns, to scholarships, and to needy individuals, Mrs. Thompson was thrifty when it came to herself. It is reported that Geraldine's sister, Ruth, on her deathbed (in 1934) made a last request of Mrs. Babcock: "Betty, I have a little cash on hand. Will you please take it and buy your mother a new dress . . . and make her wear it!"[2] Mrs. Babcock told a reporter on her mother's ninety-fifth birthday, "To my mother money is a serious responsibility. She never indulged a penny on herself."[3]

"Her daughter Pussy used to go buy her clothes every now and then when there was some special occasion coming up and she wanted her mother to look nice," Katharine White recalls. "She always wore . . . black skirts and crêpe de Chine blouses . . . and sweaters and—unbelievable—her knee socks, on occasion. . . ."[4]

It seems that Mrs. Thompson's style of dress changed as she grew older. Photographs taken in her younger years show a beautifully dressed, elegant woman. Travers Neidlinger reflects on the subject:

I would like to think of her in the period of the twenties and thirties rather than in her later years. She moved beautifully; she had a very, very fine posture and carriage. When I close my eyes and picture her, I think of the fashions of the latter part of World War I and Mrs. Thompson getting out of her car at Fort Monmouth and going over to one of the . . . gatherings. . . .[5]

"She slowed down in her eighties . . . before that, when she dressed up . . . she got dressed up; she really was a very attractive looking woman . . . very pleasant,"[6] recalls Mr. Gilbert Manson (a former tenant at Brookdale).

Yet, even in the late fifties she did dress up for certain occasions. Miss Harding remembers taking actress Katherine Hepburn to Brookdale to meet Mrs. Thompson:

So, we went in the house. . . . They went up to tell her that we were
there. . . . She came down in a few minutes . . . in one of her tea gowns
which was black and . . . had fur trimmings . . . and shining buckles
on the shoes . . . and her jewelry . . . and her rings. . . .[7]

Geraldine Livingston Thompson at Brookdale Farm in the early thirties.

Geraldine Thompson did enjoy fine jewelry. She frequently
wore a pale green, tourmaline-jeweled chain or a string of
pearls with a ruby clasp, a marquis diamond ring, a watch
or two, and—in her later years—a "Roma" pin.

Katharine Elkus White remembers:

Mrs. Thompson was tremendously ambitious and energetic physically.
And she used to get up early in the morning and run around the track,
with her knickers (she wore knickers, which were not in those days
considered stylish, and white blouses usually). And then always one of
her beautiful diamond pins stuck down here somewhere [on her
blouse]. . . . And she was an amazing mixture of . . . not caring, and the
diamond pin was as handy, and it was as good as anything else. . . .[8]

Geraldine Livingston Thompson was as practical in her social and political work as in her attire. Former New Jersey Senator Richard R. Stout likes to refer to her as a "practical idealist." "If something she was interested in was about to be defeated," Mr. Stout explains,

> . . . she would get very practical politically. She would buttonhole people and go call them on the phone. . . . When you told her the political side, the practical side, she understood immediately. She was very quick to understand the politics of the situation. Now she wasn't really guided by [politics] ; if she thought she could overcome [it], she'd probably do it.[1]

Mr. Stout remembers an incident that took place in the fifties when, during Governor Robert B. Meyner's administration, a new state prison was being proposed in Arneytown (in Central New Jersey):

> There was a group of people . . . who opposed the establishment of the state prison near their home. . . . Mrs. Thompson was pretty much for this thing. . . . Mrs. Hildebrand (it was a name very close to it)—a woman representative of the Quakers of that town—appeared before the state [Board of Controllers] . . . and . . . made an impassioned plea against putting the prison on the site. She broke down and cried . . . and that switched Mrs. Thompson. She told me later "that lady was so sincere and so concerned. . . ."
> She didn't vote that day, and the vote never took place after that.[2]

Several of her friends enjoy recounting the anecdote of Mrs. Thompson's taking twelve women to Eleanor Roosevelt's New York apartment for lunch. She had called earlier, asking Mrs. Roosevelt if she could bring eight women for lunch to discuss a speaking engagement at their national prison reform conference. Instead of the eight, Mrs. Thompson arrived with twelve guests. To appease the bewildered hostess, Mrs. Thompson waved a brown paper bag, saying, "It is all right! I've brought hamburgers for the extra four."[3]

Charles Harding, an old family friend, recalls with a smile:

> She was absolutely dynamic, and she had her mind fixed on what she

wanted to get done—to the point that nobody could escape from her, if she could catch them. She talked so fast, and would say things so fast, you couldn't possibly keep up with her. I was told that she was always going over to Trenton to beard some bureaucrat in his den, to try to get him to approve [a] project. He would say, "Mrs. Thompson, I'm sorry, I have to catch a train to Philadelphia. I have to go to the station. I'll have to see you some other day." She would say, "That's all right, I'll drive you to the station. . . ."[4]

Nobody could escape from her determined straightforwardness, not even governors. "Various governors used to have different systems on how to handle her, because she walked through all the barricades and guards,"[5] says Mrs. White. "She'd barge into the governor's office in the State House, half the time unannounced, and she'd just be like a bee going right through . . . a honeycomb,"[6] adds Richard Stout.

It has been said that as soon as Mrs. Thompson's presence was announced at the governor's office, Governor Alfred Driscoll would immediately meet her outside his office to keep the conversation short and go on with his daily schedule; otherwise she would spend the day there discussing her projects. At the dedication ceremony of the MCOSS' Geraldine L. Thompson building in Red Bank, Governor Driscoll, referring to Mrs. Thompson's accomplishments said, "I don't see, though, how you can spend so much time in the offices of the Department of Institutions and Agencies and in Monmouth County, when you spend all your time in my office."[7]

Governor Driscoll, reminiscing at Mrs. Thompson's Memorial Service in October of 1967, spoke of her as a "sage, objective, and wonderful advisor," then added, "[Once] a state trooper stopped her [outside the office] and asked her if she had an appointment. 'I do not have an appointment and I am going in,' she replied, and she marched in with an umbrella pointed at the trooper. Of course," he added, "I was delighted to see her. I was always delighted to see her."[8]

Geraldine Thompson had observed that old people tended to die within a year after retiring from work. Mrs. Babcock remembers:

6.
Perseverance

Back she went to the legislature and after fighting for seventeen years, she got them to pass a law providing old age pensions (seven years before Franklin D. Roosevelt was elected president). Now they began to live a little longer, because the small amount of money made them wanted by their younger relatives. She never, ever gave up. She would be beaten and beaten, but she could never be licked. She would always come back.[1]

Mrs. Thompson once told a reporter in reference to the state administrators, "They are there to listen when I want to say something .... I push and I prod and get a certain amount done. ... I know I open doors. If I can't open them in one place, I try another."[2]

In her strong determination to achieve her goals, Mrs. Thompson would never become discouraged when losing; on the contrary, she would use the situation to the advantage of her cause. Mrs. Babcock relates the example of the two candidates for a judgeship of a juvenile court. Mrs. Thompson supported the Republican candidate who was a "good man"; the Democratic candidate apparently did not have a good reputation. The latter won. Undaunted, Mrs. Thompson gave a great dinner party in honor of the newly-elected judge, and put him on her right at the table, in the presence of all the public officials. At the end of the party, as people were leaving, the newly-elected judge waited until he was alone with her and said, "Mrs. Thompson, I know why you have done me this honor. You want me to be a good judge!"[3]

On another occasion, she vehemently opposed the establishment of a racetrack in northern Monmouth County. When the Monmouth Park Jockey Club nevertheless was established at Oceanport, she took advantage of the situation by founding the Monmouth Park Charity Fund, which she chaired for many years. The objective of this women's organization was to raise funds through the annual Benefit Ball to assist Riverview, Monmouth Memorial (Monmouth Medical Center), and Fitkin (Jersey Shore Medical Center) Hospitals. The organization has contributed substantial amounts through the years to the three major hospitals in Monmouth County, as well as to many other charities.[4]

Mrs. Thompson's method of bringing influential people and causes together is illustrated in her working to establish the Island Beach State Park in Ocean County, New Jersey. Her correspondence file on Island Beach, dated from February 28, 1951, through July 3, 1953, relates her progress in securing the nine-mile stretch of land on Island Beach for a state park and a bird sanctuary, instead of its being sold to business interests or being used as a recreational park.

Mrs. Thompson pursued her goal for two years. Through influential friends she acquired the fifteen year planning project of New Jersey.[1] She then proposed to use the forthcoming state park at Sandy Hook "as ammunition" for the Island Beach campaign.[2] She succeeded in publicizing the "naturalistic" possibilities of the property in the press[3] and in garden clubs,[4] while through friends negotiating with the Phipps family (owners of the property) for this possibility.[5]

In June of 1953, the New York *Herald Tribune* announced that the Phipps Estate would be acquired by the State. The editor wrote: "Its acquisition as a state park, in which its rare flora and fauna will be preserved for future generations, crowns a long effort to save the island from the encroachment of commercial development."[6] Finally, in July, she took part in the presentation of the deed of sale, which she considered "a historic event."[7] Except for her friends, the public was unaware that Mrs. Thompson was instrumental in the acquisition of the state park.

She was interested basically in welfare work," explains Senator Alfred N. Beadleston, an oldtime friend of Mrs. Thompson. "Politics was a sideline, because welfare work needed the proper person in the right job at the right time. And so, I think that the welfare got her involved in politics."[1] To accomplish her welfare goals, she hand picked young people, trained them, taught them how to take "a very responsible attitude toward what it meant to be a citizen, and how [to take] government and [make] it useful to your purpose of [doing good] and creating services for people. . . ." She "made a great network of people and used [them] like

7. The Strategist

8. Recruiter of the Young

chess pieces."[2] She did not have any use for people who were apathetic, who did not care to take an active role in the community and improve conditions and services.[3]

Among the young people that Mrs. Thompson recruited were Laura Harding, Louise C. Bodman, Katharine Elkus White, Katherine Neuberger, Lutie Thompson (her daughter-in-law), Nancy Riker, Donald E. Sterner, Charles B. Harding, Raymond Eisner, Richard R. Stout, Spencer Pitts, and William B. Harding. She placed them on various committees and boards of the MCOSS, the Pet Show (Frog Town Frolic), Allenwood Tuberculosis Hospital, the state penitentiaries and reformatories, and the State Psychiatric Hospital at Marlboro. She had an uncanny way of recognizing talent in people, of looking for the best in them and giving them responsibilities, even if it required her to cede her position to a younger person. And the young always learned from her and her philosophy.

When Richard R. Stout was starting in civic and political activities, she told him,

I like your attitude, but let me tell you one thing: no matter what happens, never get disillusioned; always keep your hope up, because it will work out. Never become cynical. That's the worst thing you can do; and never lose your illusion as to what can be done.[4]

How did she succeed in making people work as volunteers for her causes? ". . . I think she had a very rare quality," says Katherine Neuberger, "to get people to work for her because she did not superimpose herself after she gave them something to do. She could delegate authority and when she gave someone something to do, she'd let them do it the way they wanted to without interference."[5]

9. Humor

The reason why she was so great to work with on what I call 'heavy duty,'" Laura Harding explains, "was because she made it all so much fun. There was never anything that was dreary or boring . . . around her. It was either terribly challenging . . . terribly interesting, or something to be explored, or she'd be ridiculously funny."[1] She recalled an MCOSS gathering held on the occasion of the Bodman Foundation's donating a generous amount to one of the health centers; Laura Harding, as the president of MCOSS had to make a speech of thanks:

... I was very nervous ... and had the speech all carefully written out. And I stood up and ... started to read this. ... She was sitting in the audience, and she looked up at me and ... said, "Are you reading that?" Right in front of about three hundred people. So, I thought, "Incredible!" And I said, "Better to read it, than to not know what I'm saying!" It brought on such a reaction, that a great many people came and said that they felt sorry for me. And a great many other people thought it was funny. And then it became an act .... Whenever I spoke, and she was sitting in the audience, she would start this needling. And it was wonderful. It relaxed me totally.[2]

Charles Harding remembers going to a meeting of a group of Republican county leaders at the courthouse in Freehold— his first experience of such a meeting. "She got up and made a speech which was the funniest thing I ever heard. She had everyone rolling in the aisles. She had been kidding all these people who were actually taking their jobs fairly seriously."[3] She was in her eighties at the time.

"... She had a pretty good sense of humor. ... She had that little smile around her face ... [when] she was about to zing somebody. Oh, she knew what she was doing,"[4] comments Richard Stout.

Mrs. Thompson is remembered by all as being punctual despite her heavy schedule and various activities. She was on time no matter how inconvenient the weather, and was always prepared for the unexpected. On the day when a testimonial dinner was given in her honor at the Stacy-Trent Hotel in Trenton, she "ordered" her daughter, Elisabeth Babcock, to bring with her a showcase of southern marsh birds in their natural habitats and six hundred Audubon Society pamphlets on the species.

The evening came to conclusion, leaving Mrs. Babcock with the paraphernalia, wondering,

*10.
Punctual,
Prepared,
and Ever
Gracious*

Why the case and pamphlets from Audubon? Like any good general, if, at the age of eighty-four, she could not muster her forces to breach the ramparts and plant the flag of hope, then a secondary diversion had to exist to "save the day."

Though I had not received an order to be prepared for a talk on birds of the marshes and my mother well knew her daughter was not versed about birds, she also knew that, were the diversion necessary, calling upon her daughter—who couldn't do it and, would so say with merriment—just might save the party from ending on a note of sadness.[1]

When Travers Neidlinger was asked what he considered Mrs. Thompson's outstanding accomplishment through the years, he replied, "Remaining a gracious lady!"[2] She had the graciousness to admit her own mistakes. She once told a reporter in 1940, "I fought the appointment of a man in this county to a judgeship tooth and nail. I fought it every way I knew how. I honestly believed he was the wrong person for the job. The majority ruled and his appointment went through. He has made one of the finest judges this county has ever had and each morning I wake up and thank God that there are people who have the foresight and vision to live up to their convictons."[3]

Senator Beadleston explains how Mrs. Thompson got her own way. "She was willing to spend a great deal of her time and her energy and her money to back up her convictions. And since she was up before you were up and since she went to bed after you went to bed, she was always the winner."[4] Richard Stout adds, "She had influence, she had friends who had influence, and she was on the side of the angels. . . ."[5]

11. Public Health and Welfare

Monmouth County Organization for Social Services (MCOSS), Allenwood Tuberculosis Hospital, and Marlboro State Psychiatric Hospital represent major accomplishments in Geraldine Thompson's long career in public health and welfare. This career began to gather momentum in 1911 when Mrs. Thompson contributed to the funding of a survey of the New Jersey Poor Laws.[1] A year later, she gathered a group of influential friends to form the Monmouth County branch of the State Charities Aid and Prison Reform Association of New Jersey,[2] a private organization that worked for more humane and efficient administration of public institutions and public assistance.

At the time, the jail was Monmouth County's only institution, community health and welfare services were few, and children were lodged in the jails. Typhoid fever and tuberculosis were widespread, school attendance was spotty, and school health programs were virtually unknown.[3] The County branch of the State Charities Aid and Prison Reform Association was interested in the control of tuberculosis. Adopting the slogan, "No Uncared for Tuberculosis in Monmouth County," the organization worked to establish a county tuberculosis hospital. The Board of Chosen Freeholders stated at a hearing that if conclusive evidence were shown of the need for such a hospital, and if the taxpayers supported it, "it would be their duty to build it." Both Colonel and Mrs. Thompson were influential in the founding of Allenwood Sanatorium in 1921. Mrs. Thompson served as president of the Board of Managers until 1951 and continued to be active even after that time.[4] In 1967, the sanatorium was named Geraldine L. Thompson Hospital.

During MCOSS' first year, the field work was done by volunteer social workers, who with Mrs. Thompson worked from a small office in Red Bank. A year later, a county nurse was employed to help meet the increasing health needs of the county. In the beginning, the organization also dealt with juvenile delinquency and sponsored and financed a child study program at Rutgers University. When the value of the program was demonstrated, the program's expenses were carried by public funds, following passage of a bill in the state legislature (as so often happened with projects sponsored by MCOSS and Geraldine L. Thompson).[6]

In 1918, the State Charities Aid and Prison Reform Association was dissolved and the Monmouth branch became the Monmouth County Organization for Social Services, Inc. In 1920, the organization was deputized by the State Department of Institutions and Agencies to cooperate with the

Department in the county; Mrs. Thompson had been influential in the passage of legislation establishing this state
department.[7]

Geraldine Thompson served on the board of MCOSS as
president from its formation to 1952. When—at the age of
eighty—she stepped down, she was succeeded by Louise C.
Bodman. Mrs. Thompson, however, continued to attend
Board meetings as president emeritus.[8] Her friend Eleanor
Roosevelt wrote in her "Showing the Way" column:

> There is one county in New Jersey—Monmouth—which I think does
> an exceptionally good job through its social services, and this is largely
> due to an outstanding citizen. Mrs. Lewis Thompson has had a hand in
> all the welfare organizations of the state, but, as she lives in Monmouth
> County, that county's organization for social service reflects her interest
> and personality . . . .
>
> She cares about people and this interest at home has taken her to her
> State Capitol and to Washington, D.C.
>
> . . . Mrs. Thompson, of course, could not do her work alone and she
> has had splended co-operation. But she gives inspiration and energy and
> courage such as few citizens give to welfare work of their communities.[9]

MCOSS handled widely varying social service responsibilities until the county government took over the work and
centralized it. In 1923, the organization was authorized to do
parole work involving field service for the State Home for
Boys (Jamesburg); State Home for Girls (Allaire); the State
Reformatory for Women (Clinton); the State Training
Schools (Lisbon, Woodbine, Totowa and Vineland); the
State Village for Epileptics at Skillman; and the State Hospitals. By 1949, the parole work of all the correctional
institutions was transferred to the State Department's Parole
Division.[10]

In 1931, following a study of the need for a county welfare house, the Welfare House was built in Freehold. Its
cornerstone was laid by Mrs. Thompson, since MCOSS "had
done much to make the establishment of the Welfare House
possible."[11] During the war years, public health nurses served
as health and welfare counselors at the various draft boards.

After the war, with the cooperation of other agencies, MCOSS proposed a health program for veterans.[12]

Nursery schools were established by MCOSS in 1929, and they continue, independently, to the present. Affiliation in public health nursing was established with general hospitals in 1932 and continues to date. In 1932, the social service department was established at Fitkin Memorial Hospital in Neptune with two thirds of the payroll paid by MCOSS. In 1949, the hospital administrators recognized the value of the service and carried the program independently.[13]

Through her association with MCOSS, Mrs. Thompson contributed to the improvement of the State Psychiatric Hospital at Marlboro by supporting the establishment of individual health care units and by assigning a corps of trained volunteers to assist the staff. Again through MCOSS, she helped a number of tubercular patients find proper care and treatment in Allenwood Sanatorium and other hospitals in New Jersey.[14] She also recognized the health needs of the migrant population in Monmouth County, and founded the Migrant Farm Workers' School, which provided education, clothing, food, and bus transportation for the students.[15]

In 1950, through the hard work of fund raising, MCOSS was able to purchase a building at 141 Bodman Place, Red Bank, and move from its original location on Pearl Street. On June 1, 1950, an outdoor ceremony took place at the new location, and the building was dedicated in Geraldine Thompson's honor.[16]

Once a small enterprise, MCOSS has grown to have an annual operating budget of over two-and-a-half million dollars. It has five health care centers in Monmouth County, serving fifty-one out of fifty-three communities. It is affiliated with various hospitals and institutions, such as Marlboro, Allenwood (still providing care for the comparatively few tubercular patients), Riverview Hospital, and Jersey Shore and Monmouth Medical Centers. It provides health care for the sick and the disadvantaged in their homes, for tubercular patients, for children, for maternity patients and the newborn; it has preventive programs for early detection of cancer, for the emotional and physical problems of senior citizens, and for mental illness. And all this is provided with little or no financial burden on the patient.[17]

As it was during Geraldine L. Thompson's active days, MCOSS is still the largest home health agency in New Jersey, one of the largest in the United States, and one of the most studied[18] —indeed a tribute to a great pioneer.

12.
Juvenile
Justice
and
Prison
Reform

Geraldine Thompson felt that as president emeritus of MCOSS she would have more time to devote to her work on the Board of Control of the State Department of Institutions and Agencies. Her first objective, she said, was to help establish "another summer school for the children of seasonal laborers—as she preferred to call the migrant workers—in South Jersey."[1]

She was interested at this point in the emotional and educational welfare of the young, especially juvenile delinquents, an interest that she was able to pursue through her position on the Board of Control. She was appointed to the board in 1918—the first woman named to an official state board.[2] She served eight consecutive terms from 1918 to 1957—the only person ever to serve on the board continuously—being appointed by both Democratic and Republican governors. Even when she announced in 1957 (at age eighty-five) that she would not accept another eight-year term, she did not retire from her interests. As an emeritus member, she continued to attend the monthly meetings of the board; once a week, she visited the children's shelter and the county jail in Freehold, state institutions for children and youth throughout New Jersey,[3] and the juvenile court at Freehold, to "rescue delinquents."[4]

Mrs. Thompson believed that psychiatric care of young law offenders should be incorporated with various other responsibilities of the Department of Institutions and Agencies.[5] She also believed that delinquent youth needed the support of the more fortunate people in order to adjust to society. She once related the incident of the boy from the State Home for Boys at Jamesburg whom she allowed to swim in her pool. "It brought a miraculous change over that boy," she remarked, "almost overnight."[6] She is reported as having said on the same occasion, "I'd love it if we could set up something for our youth in Monmouth County," then added, "We're going to start a new center for delinquent girls at Allaire. If we can do the right thing for the girls, perhaps we can get people to understand what delinquency really is and what problems young people face today."[7]

In 1960, she set up a free psychiatric service for Lincroft and Navesink public elementary school children. She matched a state appropriation to make up seventy-five thousand dollars for a professional team—a psychiatrist, a psychologist, a social case-worker, and a remedial reading teacher —to treat disturbed children.[8]

Geraldine Thompson and Eleanor Roosevelt at a dinner in 1957.

Geraldine Thompson shared a great many of Eleanor Roosevelt's interests in social welfare. In 1959, at a gathering of sixty-six government, education, and welfare leaders at Brookdale—a good example of Mrs. Thompson's ability to bring various officials and causes together—Mrs. Roosevelt, the guest speaker, urged the state officials to revaluate the state educational program, particularly in the area of mentally disturbed children. Mrs. Thompson had called the meeting to discuss problems of mentally disturbed and socially maladjusted children. Discussions centered around a bill sponsored by then Assembly Minority Leader Alfred N. Beadleston "which would establish county supervision of . . . special programs for emotionally and socially maladjusted pupils."[9] The bill, then waiting Governor Robert Meyner's signature, was later ratified. Mrs. Roosevelt also asked the state legislature to think about a program of screening pre-school children.[10]

Senator Beadleston said that early diagnosis would save taxpayers millions of dollars in rehabilitation costs. He believed that emotionally disturbed children are "without doubt" the future delinquents.[11]

Beside contributing much of her time to prison reform, Mrs. Thompson made financial donations and gifts for specific purposes. These are not well documented, because she so often gave contributions without publicity. In 1963, she donated a ten-passenger bus to be used for transporting Marlboro's child patients to outside activities. To the Jamesburg State Home for Boys, she donated one thousand dollars in 1962 for the repair of the swimming pool. The superintendent of the Home wrote to Mrs. Thompson, saying that "the therapeutic value of getting wet" was something "without which [they] could not operate successfully."[12]

Mrs. Thompson also donated a swimming pool to the State Diagnostic Center at Menlo Park. Laura Harding remembers the dedication ceremony with officials surrounding the pool:

. . . and then the attendants started to march off these kids, when all of a sudden, there was a splash. One of the biggest boys had jumped into the pool. There was horror on the faces of everybody. The attendants said, "Well, we'll have to discipline this boy!" As we were all marching away from the pool, I walked up to the boy and said, "Why did you do it?" And he pointed at Mrs. Thompson and said, "She dared me."

I thought, "They shouldn't punish him. We'll have to tell everybody why he did it, because, after all, she'd just given the pool, and if she dared him to jump in it, it was like an order."[13]

Also for the State Home for Boys at Jamesburg, she set up

a scholarship and research program at Rutgers University, in order to provide psychiatric and psychological care at the reformatory. In a letter to Mrs. Lewis W. Jones of Rutgers University on December 10, 1952, she wrote:

I think the background of the adolescent and the resulting elements in his personality must be more clearly understood and evaluated before building units are established—for certain types of boys and girls. . . .[14]

In 1965, she donated stock certificates valued at more than six thousand dollars to the State Department of Institutions and Agencies. It was called the "Geraldine L. Thompson Fund." The annual interest, two hundred fifty dollars, was meant to assist a ward of the state in paying his or her college expenses.[15]

In 1943, she was appointed a consultant to the Prison Industries Branch of the War Production Board. Subsequently, she received an award of merit for "outstanding service" to the nation, in recognition of her contribution to a program which mobilized prison industries for the war effort.[16]

Very affectionate and understanding with children, she donated two ponies to the State Home for Boys at Jamesburg for the youngsters who needed "something to care for, to love." She believed that by returning the youngsters to nature, many of their problems could be analyzed and solved.[17]

In 1959, she gave fifteen thousand dollars to the Department of Institutions and Agencies for the State Diagnostic Center at Menlo Park.[18] She allowed eighteen hundred dollars of her donation to be used in 1961 for landscaping at the State Home for Girls at Allaire. This, she thought, "would give the Diagnostic Center management a sense of comradeship and closeness to what the Turell Building Unit (at Allaire) [was] trying to do."[19]

In May of 1957, the graduating class of the Reformatory for Women at Clinton dedicated its commencement exercises to Geraldine L. Thompson, who had by then just announced her retirement from the Board of Control.[20] A testimonial dinner was held at the Stacy-Trent Hotel in Trenton on

May 17 for this "noblest citizen," commemorating her thirty-nine years of service on the State Board of Control. Among the three hundred guests were Governor Robert B. Meyner, former Governor Alfred E. Driscoll, and Mrs. Eleanor Roosevelt.

This proved to be one of the several occasions when Mrs. Thompson did not use her prepared speech. Elisabeth Babcock relates her recollections of this occasion:

I do not remember anything in this speech [draft] being said — she knew her audience was in the hollow of her hand. The past was never mentioned. First, she made them laugh until they wept, then she raised their sights to the future, the needs, the challenges, the great opportunities . . . the ever changing ways to serve those most in need. Perhaps it could be said she came close to opening the Heavens for her audience.

. . . It was a great speech. It had nothing to do with her, but everything to do with her vision, her faith, her love, her delicious sense of humor.[21]

Mrs. Thompson's intended, but unspoken speech read:

And when one is ending a career, one naturally feels the things left undone, as well as the things one was permitted to do. As the poet said, "and the little more and how much it is, and the little less and what worlds away." But I do find satisfaction in trying to report on what I have seen and what I was permitted to see done in New Jersey, in our department to open doors to one's brother man — which is really opening a door for oneself.[22]

13.
Liberation,
Women,
and
Politics

She was an extraordinary human being," Katherine Neuberger comments. "She was a 'women's libber' before the word 'liberation' came into our dictionary. She believed that women had the right and should go outside their homes and do work for the betterment of human beings. She believed that politics was a method of getting a better standard of living for people."[1]

In 1927, while still a Republican national committeewoman (elected in 1924), Mrs. Thompson encouraged women to go into politics:

Politics is a fine adventure. The best women must go into it. They will have to choose, however, between power that comes easily through patronage and fighting for the higher standards of political philosophy which will bring about the greatest ultimate success.[2]

In 1931, as a committeewoman from Monmouth County at the Republican State Convention, Geraldine L. Thompson opened her address with the following statement:

I have been given my subject for a short address today: "Women in Politics"

My first question is how shall we punctuate this caption? Shall it be a period to indicate a statement of simple fact—shall it be a question mark to suggest doubt—or an exclamation point—perhaps two or three —to mean that we are facing an important event in our forward march —or might we simply put a dash to imply that there is to be a future of still more promise and interest.[3]

Then, to answer her question, she turned to the fifth plank of the Republican platform (of New Jersey) which stated that it recognized "the appointment to office and in party councils" of women who have contributed to the success of the party and to the cause of good government, and added, "A generous hand of fellowship I would say—a promise of good things to come."[4]

As if taking women's role in politics for granted, she didn't mention women again in her speech, but talked about the party platform, political principles, the two party system, prohibition, and the role of the press.

Back in 1927, she had expressed her views of the women's suffrage movement (which had culminated in the passage of the Nineteenth Amendment in 1920, granting women the right to vote):

Great good has come of suffrage. . . . Women have taken the cover off pretty nearly everything in political procedure. That is woman's nature. She is always opening packages. She has disclosed what is happening in politics as it has never been disclosed before.[5]

Geraldine Thompson trusted women's intellectual and instinctual qualities and encouraged young women to hold board offices. However, there is no evidence that she took an active part in the suffrage movement, as her sister, Mrs. Margaret Norrie, had done. She considered "public welfare" as being the backbone of the "higher standards of political philosophy." In her own words, she "slid into politics through her welfare work. . . ."[6]

Geraldine L. Thompson entered politics in 1917, three years before women were permitted to vote. In 1923, she attended the Republican National Convention as the first woman delegate from New Jersey. In 1927, she decided not to run again for office, stating that "she had been 'shocked' by the 'disloyalty' and 'hypocrisy' of professional politicans interested only in patronage and personal power."[7]

She assured the press, "Please do not think that I believe the political situation hopeless. It is only that to carry on requires more than I have to give just now." Family obligations required more of her time and her strength, and she said, "I feel I cannot give that constructive attention to national politics which I think is due from the leaders of the party."[8]

Despite her refusal to run for office, she continued to be active on the county and state committees. She attended, as a delegate or an alternate, every Republican National Convention from 1920 to 1952, when at the age of eighty she was the oldest woman delegate. She continued to hold office as State Republican Committeewoman until 1961, when she ceded her seat to Katherine Neuberger.[9] When in 1931 she ran for county committeewoman, her opponents, taking advantage of her resignation, misrepresented her views on politics in an attempt to intimidate her. At the height of the campaign in May, she remarked, "I was supposed to have said, back in 1927, that 'politics is dishonest.' I did not say that. I said that there is dishonesty in politics, and I challenge anyone to dispute that statement."[10]

A staunch Republican, she loyally voted for all Republican presidential candidates even if she did not approve of them. In 1952, she vigorously opposed a high-ranking Republican as presidential candidate, and she said to a reporter, "And you could say I said so, except that I will have to back him if he is nominated, which I sincerely hope he is not."[11]

The state officials, in their turn, recognized Mrs. Thompson. In the late 1940's, when the ninety-two delegates met to revise the State Constitution, Mrs. Thompson at seventy-five was invited "as an official regular" to "check the motive" and protect her "interests." Governor A. Driscoll publicly referred to her as the "ninety-third delegate."[12]

During the Prohibition years—1920 to 1933—she was active in advocating the Eighteenth Amendment, seeing a moral issue in it. She held that "moral victories" were won through "physical fitness,"[13] and that alcohol, like habit-forming drugs, was "the greatest enemy to the good and the beautiful that we have."[14] Although the Eighteenth Amendment became a major issue in many elections, polarizing Republicans and Democrats, Mrs. Thompson stuck to her principles; her friends remember that through the years she never served liquor in her home.

In an effort to bring harmony to her political party, Geraldine Thompson organized a "peace Conference" at Brookdale in 1931. There were representatives of the Republican Good Government Club (organized after the party fight of 1928 and headed by Mrs. Thompson) and of the Monmouth County Republican Women's Club, headed by her opponent, Mrs. Marie Linburn. Mrs. Thompson accepted the presidency of the M.C.R.W.C. as a first step toward harmony: she even saw the possibility of merging the two clubs, stating that

Unofficial organization was the best method of discovering, developing and recognizing leadership, a recruiting ground for both the official and unofficial leadership among women, and also a way of bringing young women into positions of responsibility.[15]

Mrs. Thompson was also a member of the Women's Law Enforcement Committee, the New Jersey Council of Republican Women, and the Monmouth County Federation of Republican Women, which she founded in 1930.[16]

The late William B. Harding, one of the "thousands of 'victims' whom [Mrs. Thompson] trained for leadership," explained her philosophy of democracy in a newspaper article. He wrote:

> Geraldine Thompson has a deep, abiding faith in democracy and is a dedicated foe of autocracy, bureaucracy, [and] excessive centralization of power. But she is a realist and knows that to carry the banner of democracy, which so many do only as a slogan, is an empty gesture. "In order to have democracy you have to work at it and fight for it day and night, or it will slip away from you," she says.
>
> As she sees it, in every organization there is a perpetual war going on between those who would like to centralize power and those who wish to decentralize it. There are, of course, strong arguments on both sides; but Mrs. Thompson believes that in public institutions the widest possible public participation in the decision-making process is vital to the democratic system, that citizens who are willing to let someone else run everything for them soon lose the power to her [sic].[1]

Mrs. Thompson also believed that it was the duty of every citizen to take an interest in politics and make the party of his choice as reputable and representative as possible.

Katharine Elkus White remembers that the Democratic and Republican State Committees always met, by law, on the same day in Trenton. Mrs. Thompson would ask Mrs. White to drive her to Trenton, where they would go to their separate political meetings and return home together, "which was a wonderful example of the two party system working together." Mrs. White also recalls that Mrs. Thompson would occasionally call her and say, "Katharine, you have to serve on this committee to make the balance of power. We have to have a Democrat." "She was very friendly with me," says Mrs. White. "She was friendly with Judge Ackerson and Mrs. Ackerson, who were good Democrats. . . ."[2]

Geraldine Thompson's bipartisan friendships extended as far as the White House. Elisabeth Babcock describes one legendary White House supper:

> In 1938, Geraldine L. Thompson was a house guest at the White House. A convention on parole was taking place in Washington. She

arrived Sunday evening—Mrs. Roosevelt was out of town. The President, Mr. and Mrs. Elmhirst, Mr. Michael Straight, the President's secretary, and Mrs. Thompson were served supper in the small dining room. The President immediately held forth on parole.

Mrs. Thompson interrupted, "Franklin, what you have been saying is quite incorrect." Nothing daunted, the President picked up where he left off and pursued his theme.

Mrs. Thompson interrupted once again, "Franklin, stop. You know nothing about parole." The President did not like this at all. His secretary looked alarmed.

Mrs. Thompson looked up at her kid brother's lifelong friend. She saw he looked grim. She tapped him on the shoulder, "Dear Franklin, never forget I am your Majesty's most loyal opposition."

She looked so small, so sweet and gentle, the President relaxed and took over the conversation for the rest of the evening, on many subjects.[3]

In 1931, a Newark *Evening News* article explained Mrs. Thompson's fair-mindedness in politics:

Mrs. Thompson is not afraid to speak a kind and true word for the Democrats. Democrats, she says, are more humane than Republicans; "somehow, we must admit, they have a feeling of kinship for the man on the street and recognize his problems better than our leaders.

"The Republicans excel, of course, in matters of statesmanship and appreciation of problems relating to the city as a whole.

"There is nothing angelic about Republicans or devilish about Democrats. They are just groups of people, one of which puts more emphasis on human relations and the other stresses material affairs. The country needs them both to keep from being either too hard-boiled or too sentimental."[4]

A short speech she gave in 1931 seems relevant today:

A wise parent tries to inculcate, establish, foster principles of conduct, courageous attitudes of mind, hoping that when independent decisions must be made the children will show wisdom, courage, and discretion. There are often surprises in family life. One has most satisfactory, affectionate conferences with one's children. They leave the rooms with shining, happy faces—set for action—and the action which ensues is a complete surprise and sometimes a shock to the parents. This seems as it should be.

This sense of confidence in good things is the best gift one generation can make to the succeeding one. The same is true in politics. Not pressure, not heat in leadership, not even too much stress and hurry, certainly no sense of confusion, but rather good will within the party and among party candidates will build for the happiness of the largest number of people.

Candidates . . . will come and go . . . but the institution of democratic government will go on forever.[5]

15. Nature, Children, and Scouting

As Geraldine Thompson advanced in age, she turned more and more toward nature, toward the physical and psychological development of children, and toward the preservation of the family structure. In 1964, she told a reporter, "I think we've got to make the world over. . . . We must protect the family and make the boys and girls understand things as they approach maturity . . . . We've got to use the past to help the future."[1]

After spending a two-week holiday in 1950 at the Audubon Camp at Muscongus Bay, Maine, Mrs. Thompson often talked about nature, about the furtherance of the ideals of the National Audubon Society, and about her disappointment that she couldn't get every bird in Monmouth County to visit the feeding station on her Brookdale Farm.[2]

In 1958, Mrs. Thompson donated a "handsome bird chart in full color," depicting American birds, to every Audubon Junior Club; each chart was accompanied by a teaching outline entitled, "A Bird Study for Spring," for teachers and youth leaders.[3] According to a note from a friend at the National Audubon Society, the project received a "wonderful response."[4]

In April of 1962 Mrs. Thompson, just turned ninety and recovering from a serious operation, participated in a tree planting ceremony at the Middletown Village School with members of the school's Junior Audubon Society. The editor of the *Courier* reported the ceremony, describing the way Mrs. Thompson talked to the children as human beings, fascinated them with stories of Teddy Roosevelt and Eleanor Roosevelt, and aroused more interest in "the children's minds than any history book, no matter how profusely illustrated, ever could."[5]

She believed in teaching children through first-hand information. In 1954, with her grandson, Peter Van Gerbig, she donated live animals—"Chuckles," the woodchuck, and a flying squirrel among others—to the American Museum of Natural History's Natural Science Center for Young People. She wanted New York children to get acquainted with, to touch, and to learn from live animals. The exhibition's theme was "Preparing for Winter" (hibernation).[6] According to Mrs. Babcock, "It was loved by the children and was a mad success."[7]

In 1963, Mrs. Thompson underwrote a program and provided scholarships for many Girl Scout leaders and teachers to go to the Audubon Camps in Connecticut, Maine, Wisconsin, and Wyoming. Charles Harding wrote to her acknowledging this fine gesture and thanking her for her five-thousand-dollar donation to the newly-forming Monmouth Museum (at this time planned for Holmdel Park). Mr. Harding expressed hope that the trained teachers would bring the children to the museum and the park "to derive benefit from what we will be able to offer."[8] In another letter he wrote: "... the concept of the Museum presents a wonderful opportunity for the community. Our aims will complement your own desire to fill the recreational need of the county's youth...."[9]

If Geraldine L. Thompson had seen the actual museum and the adjoining nature center established on her estate, she undoubtedly would have felt great satisfaction. She often said that children should be given the opportunity to study nature, because the youngster who isn't particularly enchanted by football will know that it is all right for him to climb a tree and find a bird's nest.

Geraldine Thompson was one of the founders of scouting in Monmouth County in 1917;[10] in recognition, the Monmouth Council of Boy Scouts of America presented her their first Beaver award.[11] She always supported the scouts and their ideals, and in 1954, on the forty-fourth anniversary of scouting in America, she hosted a Camporee at her farm.[12]

In that same year, while launching a ship of the United States Merchant Marine, she surrounded herself with scouts as she opened her speech with the following remark:

... a grateful ancient mariner—and obviously an ancient one—has come today to dedicate a ship, the *Silver Mariner*. She has chosen as her lady in waiting a Mariner Girl Scout ... also a gentleman in waiting, a boy Sea Scout ... and two younger members of God's children. And we are glad to have a Cub Scout and a Brownie Scout with us. To me this Cub Scout is like a little Samuel who might be saying to the sea, "Speak, Lord, for Thy servant heareth." [13]

In 1958, in recognition of her contribution to scouting throughout her long life, the Monmouth County Boy Scout camp at Forestburg, New York, was dedicated in her honor.[14] And in 1964 she was honored with a Girl Scout statuette in recognition of the scholarships she had provided for Girl Scout leaders.[15] She also received various other honorary plaques from local scout troops.

16. Education: Assistance Given and Honors Received

Recognizing the need to assist black students in obtaining higher education, in 1952 Mrs. Thompson initiated the IKE scholarship (in honor of presidential candidate Dwight D. Eisenhower), in the amount of one thousand dollars for an outstanding black high school graduate. Mrs. Thompson hoped that the Republican organizations would take the responsibility for its funding in subsequent years.[1]

In 1955, she provided funds for Dr. Frederick M. Raubinger, New Jersey Commissioner of Education, to take a trip to Europe and Russia to study school systems there. Her major concern at this point was learning the reasons why "children get into trouble at school," and learning ways of keeping the children out of her "department" (of Institutions and Agencies).[2]

Aware that a good education involved more than the three "R's," Mrs. Thompson once told a reporter:

The period of youth has a sensitivity about it which can destroy itself if not properly cared for. ... Schools have to give more cooperation and uplift—not only things you get out of books. I think the world is going to have to know more about matters of heart.[3]

In recognition of Mrs. Thompson's contribution to education, the Middletown Township Board of Education, in 1962, named a new school for her. The Thompson school is situated on a thirty-acre tract, at the corner of Dwight and Middletown-Lincroft Roads.[4]

In recognition of her work in the fields of public welfare and social reform, she was awarded an honorary degree of Master of Philanthropy by the New Jersey College for Women (later known as Douglass College) of Rutgers University, in 1931. In a letter preceding the awarding of the degree she wrote to Dean Mabel S. Douglass:

I must humbly confess that I have no academic regalia nor, which to me is far more distressing, any College or University degrees; as a matter of fact I have no diplomas from schools of any sort, kind, and variety!

My scholastic career can be described only as it occurred under tutors, governesses, and in private schools.[6]

Friends remember Mrs. Thompson as an avid reader of materials relating to her work in social welfare and prison reform, and of poetry, especially the Elizabethan, Victorian, and American poets. When a reporter asked her what she would advise people who sought inspiration, she replied, "[Read] the poets and the prophets."[7]

In 1959, Monmouth College awarded to Geraldine Thompson the first honorary Doctor of Letters degree in its history, citing her lifelong and continuing devotion to the betterment of society.[8]

17. Planning the Future of Brookdale

Because the land where Brookdale Community College is located today was willed by Mrs. Thompson to her son, Lewis S. Thompson, Jr., she did not have any part in planning its future disposition. She did, however, plan the future of her own Brookdale estate (now Thompson Park), adjoining her son's property.

The last portrait of Geraldine Livingston Thompson, taken in 1954 at age 82.

Documents indicate that in 1959 Mrs. Thompson was approached by members of a Quaker group and by officials from Rutgers University, both of whom saw possibilities of building on her estate.[1] Former New Jersey State Highway Commissioner E. Donald Sterner remembers being instrumental, with a few friends, in persuading her to will the estate instead to Monmouth County. Mr. Sterner, who considered Mrs. Thompson a second mother, "at least a political mother,"[2] recalls her thinking that Rutgers with its large budget would tie Brookdale into its program. If Rutgers had acquired Brookdale, he notes, it would not have been an institution reaching lower-income students, as Brookdale Community College came to be. He believes that had Mrs. Thompson seen how the architects set classes in the former stables and preserved the architectural character of the farm, she would have been very pleased.[3]

Early in 1960, Mrs. Thompson was preoccupied with the future possibilities of Brookdale. On a newspaper clipping in her files are her handwritten notes that read: "40 acres to county [sic] Park and Recreation Department for (playground) children of Lincroft. Brookdale 225 acres inc. 17 bldgs. to county of Mon. as park and wildlife preserve."[4]

A few years earlier, she had told a reporter, "We've got to live with nature. The children have to feel the ground beneath them and go out in the woods and see the trees and birds."[5]

In 1961, Mrs. Thompson informed a reporter that her greatest desire was to turn her Brookdale estate into a county park. She added, "I would like nothing better than to know that Brookdale in the future would be an open place for chil-

Elisabeth Thompson Babcock at her mother's memorial service on October 9, 1967 at Christ Episcopal Church in Middletown.

dren and for animals because they have a place here, too . . . .
I would want it to be under the control of the county and
open to all." However, she told him, she would have to talk it
over with her son and daughter before doing anything definite.[6]

In 1964, she talked again about donating her part of Brookdale Farm to the Board of Freeholders "to be used for nothing else but children." "I'm trying to arrange for a pool for
them to swim in," she told a reporter.[7]

In 1968, a year after Mrs. Thompson's death and according
to the terms of her will, the county acquired her portion of
the estate and called it "Thompson Park."[8] At present the
Thompson Park Visitor Center (formerly the Thompson mansion) is devoted to cultural programs, and houses offices and
studios on the second floor. Plans for the future of the park
are in keeping with Mrs. Thompson's wishes.

18.
"And Gladly
She Lived"

It is impossible to document completely Geraldine Thompson's contributions to this county and state because her influence was widespread and she often worked in the background,
taking satisfaction in the outcome rather than in herself. She
accepted recognition, however, with humor and practicality.
"After all," she said, "If I'm made more important, the things
I try to do become more important too."[2]

In her later years, she was more and more confined to her
home at Brookdale. Her perception was limited to vision in
one eye, she had almost no hearing, and she had been hurt
by many losses in her family. Mrs. Babcock, describing her
mother's later period wrote:

My poor mother, he [Lewis, who died in 1964] was the darling of her
heart but she was so shattered by the death of Bill and Puss, sixteen
years before, in a way her heart was an oversoaked blotter. The blows
of fate can run out, even when they come again and again. Woe, is a
good word—when the cup of woe is filled to the brim, more woe can't
go into the cup. She was too old, too weak for anything but her lifelong
love for and trust in God. God came and refilled her loyal and devoted
heart with love and resignation.[3]

William Thompson at St. Moritz just prior to his climbing accident.

She died in the arms of her daughter on September 9, 1967, at the age of ninety-five. According to her wish, there was no formal funeral. Her body, untouched by embalming fluids, was carried in an old farm truck to the graveyard of St. James Church in Hyde Park.[4] On October 8, a memorial service was held at Christ Episcopal Church in Middletown in the presence of over two hundred friends. Her favorite prayer, attributed to St. Francis of Assissi, was said in unison:

Lord, make me an instrument of Thy peace; Where there is hatred, let me sow love; Where there is doubt, faith; Where there is despair, hope; Where there is darkness, light; and where there is sadness, joy. . . .[5]

Ten years after her death, many people who read or heard of Geraldine Thompson while she was alive remember her as a legend in her own time; the friends who have survived her remember her strong character and cheerful disposition. One wonders whether oncoming generations will ever know who stood behind all the institutions and organizations that they inevitably will take for granted. But Geraldine Thompson did not carry out her humanitarian work for her personal glorification. The state correctional institutions, MCOSS, various hospitals, Thompson Park, and—in a special sense—Brookdale Community College, symbolize today the noble ideals of this "efficient, aggressive, kind person."[7]

PART III:
BROOKDALE COMMUNITY COLLEGE

Section I:
The Founding by Joan Grantges

The spirit of Geraldine Thompson, a unique American woman, lives on in the unique American institution that now graces the land that was once Brookdale Farm. At the time of her death on September 9, 1967, Mrs. Thompson could not have known that within a few years Brookdale's great twenty-mare barn would house student learning stations, the stallion barn would shelter Community Services, and the "sick" barn would contain the offices of the President and administrative staff of Brookdale Community College.

But those who knew her agree that she would have been delighted that the land she and her family loved had become the home of the County College of Monmouth. She would have been pleased to hear Mrs. Katherine Neuberger, Chairman of the New Jersey Board of Higher Education, make the following evaluation: "From an architectural standpoint, Brookdale is number one. Academically, I would say it's probably in a tie with Bergen County College. . . . It's a college that I think not only this county, but the whole state would be proud of."[1]

Brookdale rates high also with Trustee William O. Fleckenstein who believes that Brookdale has a reputation in the county that is unusual for such a young institution.[2] And Ret. Major General W. Preston Corderman, who was chairman of Brookdale's Board of Trustees for eight years, feels "we have one of the finest county colleges in the state. . . ."[3]

In 1977, Brookdale radiates an ambiance that Geraldine Thompson would have approved. Brookdale Trustee Leon Zuckerman captured it when he talked about commencement at Brookdale:

There you see the melting pot, the different types of people—people in their sixties, people in their twenties—all together, getting degrees... the happy faces, particularly the older people who have never had an opportunity to go on to higher education. And here they are, getting a diploma! Some are parents and grandparents—and to see their children applaud!

And you see some of the handicapped people getting their degrees. I think the record of acceptance, the total feeling about Brookdale—being without prejudice towards race or religion—is one of the most outstanding examples of a student body that I have ever seen . . . . You can see everybody in that college family.[4]

But the beauty, the excellent academic reputation, the ambiance of Brookdale did not appear overnight; the college is the product of the persistent efforts of many people. The history of Brookdale's founding reveals the college to have had its roots in the community from the start; the institution is a true "community" college in every sense of the word.

How did it all begin? James R. Greene, who served as one of Brookdale's first trustees, says that around the time the college was getting under way there was an enormous interest in education in general in the United States.[1] For instance in the 1960 *Goals for Americans: The Report of the President's Commission on National Goals*, John W. Gardner recommended setting goals for higher education in the United States. If accomplished, these goals would bring the educational level of the general population to a point higher than that reached by any nation in history:

2. Of the People

... there should be roughly within the commuting distance of every high school graduate (except in sparsely settled regions) an institution that performs the following functions:

(a) offers two-year terminal programs for students not going on to a four-year college career.

(b) offers transfer programs for students who do wish to complete a four-year college program.

(c) serves as a technical institute for the community, serving local needs for vocational and sub-professional education.

(d) offers continuing education to adults.

Mr. Greene remembers that particularly in New Jersey there was a "feeling that college seemed to be the privilege of the middle class, the upper-middle class, and the well-to-do. There were no public universities other than Rutgers (which was expensive, far away, and unavailable to many). . . . So the State Department of Education . . . decided that [all] youngsters . . . ought to have the right . . . to start some sort of educational process beyond high school."[2]

Actually, milestones leading to the development of county colleges in New Jersey appeared as early as 1930:

1930—New Jersey State Board of Regents first recommended the state establish nine "junior colleges." (This recommendation was repeated annually through 1939.)

1950—An educational survey conducted for the State Department of Education recommended that nine community colleges be established in New Jersey.[3]

1956—*The Closing Door to College*, an abbreviated version of a State Board of Education publication, *New Jersey's Under-Graduates, 1954-73*, was widely distributed. The study examined increased enrollments in state secondary schools and "their relationship to future opportunities for New Jersey youth to gain admission to institutions of higher learning. . . ." The study warned that by 1963 the shortage of college facilities would be critical.[4]

1957—*College Opportunity in New Jersey*, a State Board of Education study, described the purpose of community colleges and stated that "certain areas of New Jersey would probably be better served by the development of two-year community colleges than by the establishment of new four-year colleges."[5] From this study the successful bond issue of 1959 was developed.

Before 1961—Several unsuccessful attempts were made by citizens' groups to establish two-year colleges in New Jersey. The experience of these groups indicated that the major deterrent to establishing two-year colleges was the lack of appropriate legislation.[6]

1961—In *Education Beyond High School: The Two-Year Community College*, the New Jersey Board of Education indicated to the governor and the legislature the extent of the need for establishing two-year institutions.[7] The study is recognized as having "laid the groundwork for legislation making possible the establishment of community colleges."[8]

April 1962—The "Strayer Report," *Needs of New Jersey in Higher Education*, cited the need to double public higher education facilities in New Jersey and recommended spending at least $134 million in added college construction by 1970.[9]

May 7, 1962—The County College Bill was enacted, to become effective July 1, 1963.

The original bill leading to the County College Act of 1963 (the legislation that enabled the Freeholders to establish county colleges), was written by Monmouth County's Dr. Joseph E. Clayton, New Jersey Deputy Commissioner of Education from 1953 to 1968. Dr. Clayton considers the late fifties a time of great importance. As he tells it,

A group of sixteen industrial leaders from the state visited Commissioner Raubinger [and Dr. Clayton] in Trenton to discuss the need for a two-year program beyond high school. These men stated that unless the state did something to provide training for people beyond high school, they were going to be compelled to look for manpower elsewhere, and with their industries leave the state of New Jersey.

As a result of that conference, the commissioner and Dr. Clayton "worked up a program and decided to appoint a committee to study the community college, technical needs, and technical institutes in the state of New Jersey."[10]

After two years that committee made an objective study of the need for two-year colleges in the state and submitted a report, *The Two-Year Community College*, to the State Board of Education. That report, Dr. Clayton says,

. . . basically outlined what developed later into the 1963 County College Act. It set up the control (the fact that the board of trustees would be appointed by the Board of Freeholders), the terms [of office] and provisions that the County Superintendent of Schools should be on that board. It was also spelled out that the first board of trustees would be appointed for staggered terms [so there would not be a complete turnover at a political whim].[11]

According to Dr. Clayton there were very few changes in the bill before it went to the legislature, where it was sponsored by Assemblyman Alfred N. Beadleston of Rumson. "There wasn't any big selling job in the legislature; they recognized there was a need and the bill passed. . . . No compromises had to be made and no amendments had to be made to it." [12]

As soon as the County College Bill passed the legislature, on May 7, 1962, counties around the state began to lay groundwork for determining the needs for county colleges in their areas. Dr. Clayton describes those early reactions:

The county college movement went, I think, far beyond what any of us had anticipated at the time we enacted the statute because there was even a greater need throughout the state than we realized when we made the study and passed the law to develop the county colleges. As a result of the law's being passed, we set up a schedule in the department . . . whereby each county would make a feasibility study, and that study would then be turned over to the department for review before the State Board of Education authorized the creation of the county college. . . . And we found . . . that when they made these studies, there was a great need for a two-year program. [13]

Citizens of New Jersey appeared eager to have their county colleges, and on September 14, 1966, the first county college in the state, Ocean County College, opened in Toms River. Later that same year Atlantic, Cumberland, and Middlesex county colleges began classes.

Superintendent of Monmouth County Schools Earl B. Garrison became familiar with the County College Act through his association with Dr. Clayton, who had been Mr. Garrison's immediate predecessor. Armed with reports and other data, Mr. Garrison was the first to propose the idea of a county college to the Freeholders. Remembering that day, former Freeholder Director Joseph C. Irwin said that "because of the number of young people in the county and the growth of our population," he felt Garrison's proposal was an opportunity for the community. He talked to the other Freeholders and found that although many were enthused about it, some wanted to be certain the people of Monmouth County were in favor of it. [14]

As a result of these early discussions, Freeholder Marcus Daly, at a regular meeting of the Board of Chosen Freeholders on June 5, 1963, offered a resolution that Superintendent of Schools Garrison make a survey to determine the feasibility of a public county college in Monmouth County.[15]

Marcus Daly's resolution was adopted, and with its acceptance began not only the determination of the need for such a college, but a great drama: Would the proposed institution become a part of Monmouth College in West Long Branch (an existing private institution) or would it be a separate and distinct institution? Through it all, one man—Joseph C. Irwin, then Director of the Board of Chosen Freeholders—was to prove himself a great statesman.

3.
The Law's
Delay

New Jersey Senator Alfred N. Beadleston was to say, "I don't know of any single person in Monmouth County who had more to do with the implementation of the [County College] Act, as far as Brookdale is concerned, than Joe Irwin."[1] But in 1963 when a letter drafted by Irwin was sent out inviting individuals to serve on the Freeholders' Study Committee being formed to determine the need for a county college, no one could have guessed from the letter's final paragraph that there ever would be such a place as Brookdale Community College:

In view of the existence of Monmouth College in our County, and in connection with our Vocational School Program, we would be very appreciative if you would consent to serve on this fact finding Committee for the County of Monmouth in connection with our Educational Programs. . . .[2]

All thirteen people originally invited to serve on the Freeholders' Study Committee accepted; Superintendent Garrison became committee chairman. The final report of the comittee, released in December, 1965, stated that at its initial meeting the committee "was in unanimous accord that the study must be thorough, accurate, and impartial."[3] As we shall see, the thoroughness and accuracy of this study were to be severely judged after its release two and one-half years later. Its impartiality was questioned when it became known that at its second meeting, the committee established the following general purposes: "(A) Establish the total county post-secondary need, and (B) Determine the role to be played by Monmouth College."[4]

Among the areas Mr. Garrison and his committee examined were county college legislation; Monmouth County school enrollment and population growth; money available and money needed; and the history of Monmouth College (which had originally been a two-year college).[5]

The Freeholders' resolution to initiate the *Study on the Need for a County College in Monmouth County* was passed June 5, 1963. The first draft of the report, however, was not ready until September 27, 1965,[6] and the final report was not given to the Freeholders until December 18, 1965. The following day, the Asbury Park *Press* reported: "Four of the five Freeholders received copies late yesterday. Copies of the report were hand delivered to the Freeholders' homes."[7] This procedure appears to indicate concern about getting the report into the hands of the Freeholders as soon as possible. If this concern existed it was well-founded, for during the two and one-half year delay the interest, and often the ire, of

Aerial view of Brookdale Farm showing the reservoir at the top and Newman Springs Road in the lower left-hand corner.

several community individuals and groups had been aroused over the idea of establishing a separate county college.

The first concerned citizen on record as making a public statement urging the establishment of a county college in Monmouth County was Paul Zar of Red Bank. On August 25, 1964, he spoke to the Greater Freehold Area Chamber of Commerce suggesting that a two-year county college be situated in the Freehold area. In 1965, Mr. Zar organized "Citizens for Monmouth Community College" to help him further his ideas.[8] Although little is documented about this committee, it appears that Mr. Zar was very active personally in spreading the word about the need for a county college. Former Freeholder Irwin says of Zar: "He was very much in favor of [the community college]."[9]

In August of 1964, Mr. Zar had written to Mr. Irwin advocating the establishment of a county college that would be separate from Monmouth College. Irwin's reply, printed in the Monmouth County publication, *The Advisor*,[10] stated:

[The Freeholders] have for many years supported the Monmouth Junior College and later the Monmouth College. The Board has established scholarship funds, loan funds, and supports the efforts of the school in

Aerial view of a portion of Brookdale Community College with two original small barns in the foreground and two large barns — one to the right and one at the top.

many other ways. We feel that Monmouth College is well satisfying the current needs in Monmouth County.

So, at this early date, Paul Zar was one of the few residents of Monmouth County who was aware of the fact that Freeholder Irwin did not favor a separate county college. In retrospect, Zar says: "Fifty million dollars of public money poured into a private college . . . didn't make any sense to me if I am going to live in this county. I didn't want the taxpayers in this county to have rent receipts. I wanted them to own the building! So I fought against it. That was the pitch." [11]

Another resident interested in the prospective county college was Elisabeth Kelley, then Legislative Chairman of the Northern Monmouth County Branch of the American Association of University Women (AAUW). In the course of her legislative work, Miss Kelley obtained literature describing the County College Act and what was being done to implement the act in the state. [12]

The state division of AAUW took up the subject of county colleges at a meeting in New Brunswick in September, 1964. Miss Kelley attended that meeting, as did Elizabeth Sanderson, then president of the Northern Monmouth Branch, and Audrie LaTowsky, chairman of the branch's Education Study Group. Miss Kelley later shared with Mrs. LaTowsky the county college materials she had obtained; she also informed local AAUW leaders of the status of the Freeholders' study, pointing out that it had been well over a year since the study was commissioned and that the committee had not yet released any information.

Given impetus by Miss Kelley's research on the county college situation, Mrs. LaTowsky and the AAUW Education Study Group laid out a plan of action. They decided, says Mrs. LaTowsky, to

. . . find out about the California system of community colleges. That's one state that has always been a great leader in education. We knew they had the community colleges there, the state colleges, and the state universities . . . and we wondered if this was a plausible route for . . . New Jersey to follow too—although we knew ours could not be free education as it is in California. But it could be that kind of pyramid system.[13]

The AAUW education group was most interested in find-out about the Freeholders' study. But regardless of how the women tried, they could not obtain any information on the status of the report. The group then decided to request information from the State Department of Education. "We found out who was the director of the two-year county college program, that was Dr. Guy V. Ferrell," says Mrs. LaTowsky,

... and we invited him to speak to our branch. . . . He was very receptive to coming down to Monmouth County to speak [at our April meeting] . . . . He was running into . . . opposition from the Freeholders and from the committee that had been appointed to study [the need for a county college] because they wanted to establish it at Monmouth College. He was very supportive of our position, which was developing at that time, that [the county college] not be established at Monmouth College; that is, it should be a separate, distinct entity.[14]

According to Mrs. LaTowsky, Dr. Ferrell proved to be very supportive of any group that would push for a county college, and felt this was the proper way rather than to have the state do the pushing. The open meeting, held in a Shrewsbury public school, was not attended by large numbers of people. However, several individuals were motivated as a result of that meeting to form a special AAUW County College Study Committee (separate from the Education Study Group) which would work at promoting the idea of a county college until it finally was established. The new group continued the attempt to obtain information on the Freeholders' Study Committee report. Mrs. LaTowsky said her committee was told that the report was not finished. "It went on and on . . . it just seemed to go on forever. We started [trying to get it] in the spring [of 1965], and it was supposed to be ready anytime, and that fall we were still trying to get copies of it . . . . I believe . . . they thought there would be opposition to the county college, and they were reluctant to get it out in the open."[15]

Mary Lou Wagner, a member of Mrs. LaTowsky's committee and president of AAUW in 1969-71, also remembers "prodding County officials . . . about what they were doing or what they planned to do about establishing [a county college] here in our county."[16]

But the AAUW committee continued to be unsuccessful in their efforts to get the Freeholders to release the report. In frustration, Mrs. LaTowsky told of her committee's activities at the May 25, 1965, meeting of the AAUW Board of Directors. After the board discussed the situation, Mrs. LaTowsky moved that

. . . the County College Special Committee be authorized to gather data and approach other groups for support, and to publicize the need for a Monmouth County college and to take whatever steps necessary to obtain the release of the report from the Freeholders.[17]

With the AAUW board's approval, Mrs. LaTowsky and her committee intensified their efforts to work for a county college. On June 6, 1965, a four-column article headlined "University Women Demand Results of College Study, Threaten Action" appeared prominently in the Asbury Park *Press.* The paper reported:

According to Mrs. Harry R. LaTowsky of New Shrewsbury . . . she had authorization to proceed with an investigation of the educational needs in the county.

"We in AAUW are in favor of a county college if the need points to this, but what are the needs?"

Mrs. LaTowsky said she tried to get the answer March 9 from Earl Garrison, head of the Monmouth County College Study Group and County Superintendent of Schools.

"Mr. Garrison told us the study was completed and the findings were on his desk, but the final report still had to be written before the details could be released."

In January, Mrs. LaTowsky asked Freeholder Marcus Daly when the report would be made known and he said, "hopefully late spring." Her latest efforts to find out the status of the study were on May 12 in a letter to Freeholder Director Joseph C. Irwin. As of Friday [June 4] she had not received a reply.

"Therefore," she said, "we in AAUW will start our own study. I would think this study would get top priority from the Freeholders."[18]

In the summer of 1965, members of Mrs. LaTowsky's committee met with members of the Jersey Shore Branch of AAUW at Monmouth College to discuss views on community colleges with David M. Espey, Registrar and Dean of Admissions. The Dean revealed that he was against having a separate institution as the county college and in favor of the idea that the county college should be established at Monmouth College. It also became clear from Dean Espey's comments that Monmouth College would not agree to an open admissions policy, and could not offer the variety of programs that Brookdale eventually did.[19]

Later Dr. William G. Van Note, President of Monmouth College, issued a statement saying that it would be far too expensive for Monmouth County to duplicate the effort in building a new college when it had all the facilities at Monmouth College to support the county college type of program. Mrs. LaTowsky says, "Of course we just laughed. We were in favor of a separate . . . institution because we wanted the technical programs Monmouth College didn't offer."[20]

Throughout the remainder of 1965, the AAUW committee met a number of times to discuss new information on community colleges. That fall, the committee announced that when the report of the Freeholders' Study Committee was made public, the AAUW committee planned a careful study of its recommendations. They followed the establishment of county colleges in other counties and continually urged the publication of the study directed by the Freeholders.[21]

Finally, on December 18, 1965, two and one-half years after the study had been authorized, the Freeholders received the hand-delivered copies of the long awaited Study Committee's report. It appears that the major cause of delay was the committee's concern for how Monmouth College would react to the study's findings. Earl Garrison, Chairman of the Study Committee, stated that

. . . one of the problems [in putting together the report] was Monmouth College . . . . We did want to have an agreement on the committee when we submitted our final report to the Freeholders. And having the President of Monmouth College [on the committee], it wasn't the easiest thing to convince him that he wasn't going to lose tremendously by having the college next door to him. . . .[22]

Mr. Garrison further explained that "the committee was aware that Mr. Irwin, who was the Director of the Board of Freeholders, was also on the board for Monmouth College. We were trying to make a smooth transition. Joe never opposed the college in any way, shape or form. He was very open-minded about it."[23]

Mr. Irwin favored a tie-in of the county college with Monmouth College as late as September 2, 1965, when an article, "Irwin Suggests Coordinating County College, Monmouth," appeared in the Asbury Park *Press*. The article reported that in an address to the Kiwanis Club in Belmar, New Jersey, Mr. Irwin had suggested "that a proposed two-year county college be coordinated with the facilities of Monmouth College. . . ." Mr. Irwin's open-mindedness, however, was apparent in the article which further quoted him as saying that "the question of whether we should have a county college at Monmouth College or build an independent college remains to be decided. . . ."

Looking back on this period from his vantage point on Brookdale's Board of Trustees in 1976, Leon Zuckerman reasoned that "if it hadn't been for the fact that Monmouth College was here, I think that Monmouth County, being the nature of the county that it is, would have moved much quicker [in getting a county college started]."[24]

Dr. Joseph I. Robinson, associate professor at Brookdale Community College, noted in a 1972 dissertation that a compromise on the Study Committee "in the face of state pressure toward the establishment of a community college in Monmouth County" was made "between the committee's pro-community-college group (which included Mr. Harold Kelly of the Red Bank *Daily Register*), and anti-community-college forces led by Dr. Van Note."[25] Arriving at this compromise must have contributed to the delay, for Dr. Van

Note was at first adamantly opposed to the notion of a community college. However, Mr. Garrison noted that "in all fairness to Dr. Van Note, he was extremely cooperative, and saw that it [the county college] was inevitable. I think all he was trying to do was to make the best arrangement. . . ."[26]

When the Freeholders' Study Committee Report was released to the public, it was evident that the voice of Monmouth College had been loud, strong, and influential. Of the ten pages in the main body of the report, more than three were devoted to information on the history, academic structure, facilities, and future enrollment capacity of Monmouth College. The study concluded that

1. Monmouth County needed a two-year post-secondary program to provide immediately for the needs of 800-1000 students.
2. Monmouth County should utilize fully the educational opportunities provided by the Junior College Division of Monmouth College.
3. There was need for increased technical education in Monmouth County.
4. "Further study should be given to acquisition of land for future development."[27]

The report recommended that the Freeholders establish a two-year county college to provide post-high school technical education to Monmouth County residents, and that the board of trustees of the county college set up an arrangement to continue the support then provided by the Freeholders and the state for county students in the Junior College Division of Monmouth College. The county college board of trustees was also asked to provide the post-high school technical education then being provided for by the County Vocational Board. The final recommendation was that the State Board of Education be petitioned to approve this so that the county would be eligible for reimbursement from the state.[28]

Reaction to the Study Committee's recommendations was swift. The first public reply was a favorable editorial, "The County College Report," appearing in the December 22,

4.
A Dignity of Its Own

1965, *Daily Register.* The editorial stated that "taking every-thing into consideration, the report's recommendations are logical and if followed, would be the speediest way to put the community college program into effect." Other, not so favor-able comments also began to be heard. Senator Eugene Bedell, then Freeholder, concluded that "it was preordained from the start that the entire intention was to use the moneys available for a county college to subsidize the education of those already attending Monmouth College, and to designate Monmouth College as the repository of our county college or community college efforts." Bedell had found the com-munity college concept something he thought "very, very worthwhile . . . and from the start had lobbied for a separate institution in Monmouth County. . . ." When that separation was not recommended in the report, Bedell says he "was highly critical of the report in the press." In his opinion what was being recommended was "an attempt to bail out Mon-mouth College, which had financial difficulties at the time."[1]

In January, 1966, William Van Note, having completed his duties on the Study Committee, apparently felt that Mon-mouth College was free to begin a vigorous campaign to per-

One of the two Brookdale Farm large horse barns before renovation.

suade county groups and individuals to support the idea of a county college tie-in with Monmouth College. One of the major thrusts of the massive public relations campaign the College was conducting at this time involved letters sent by the alumni association to all Monmouth College graduates, seeking support for using Monmouth College to provide the liberal arts program of the proposed county college. Senator Bedell, as a graduate of Monmouth Junior College, was infuriated: "I got a copy of the letter . . . made it public and raised hell about it."[2]

Dr. Van Note was anxious for the Freeholders to approve the Study Committee Report because it would mean his college was that much closer to being granted the responsibility —and the state and county funds—for the education of Monmouth County liberal arts students. His impatience was voiced in an article "Delay in College Report a Disservice: Van Note" appearing in the Asbury Park *Press*, February 11, 1966:

Delay in accepting recommendations of the Monmouth County College Study Committee would, in Dr. William G. Van Note's opinion, "be a great disservice to the youth of the county. . . . Any other direction or activity other than the recommendations of the Study Committee

The same barn now used by Brookdale Community College as the Creative Arts Center.

attempting to meet these needs is so tragically wasteful of money, of educational experience, of the resources of a $25 million educational institution now in the county, and perhaps most of all, of time, as to border on madness."

The Freeholders apparently needed more time to study the report before approving it. Joseph Irwin recalls vividly that the subject of the proposed college "would come up every time [the Freeholders] got together. And that was more than four times a month. And it would go on and on and on." They were talking about costs and how far they could go and the dealings they would have with the State of New Jersey and the Department of Education.[3]

Finally, on March 4, 1966, the Freeholders adopted the report and, as the next step in establishing the proposed institution, petitioned Dr. Frederick M. Raubinger, State Commissioner of Education, to make a study of the feasibility of a county college in Monmouth County. Freeholder Bedell voted against the report, stating in the March 16, 1966, Asbury Park *Press* that although he was not opposed to the county college, he was not in accord with the Study Committee's report whose recommendations, he believed, would be serving the interest of Monmouth College and not the intent of the College Act of 1963.

In the meantime, Audrie LaTowsky and her AAUW committee had completed a study on community colleges and were proceeding to educate and unite individuals and community groups in support of a separate two-year county college. "The AAUW's raising of the issue began to be quite a hot issue in the community. . . . The Board of Freeholders recognized that they were getting a very lively public issue on their hands," says Elinor Multer, who at that time was education writer for the *Daily Register*.[4]

Mrs. Virginia Vreeland, President of the Monmouth County Council of the League of Women Voters and a member of AAUW, knew of Mrs. LaTowsky's study and was interested in the county college issue. The two groups began to cooperate, and on March 31, 1966, AAUW presented a county college program at a meeting of the League.

The AAUW presentation to the League emphasized Monmouth County's need for a comprehensive two-year community college with facilities "so unified that they break the barrier between the technical and non-technical students." Mrs. LaTowsky presented an eight-point list of what the AAUW committee believed a county college could do:

1. Provide local higher education opportunities to thousands of qualified youth who might otherwise be denied such opportunities.
2. Enable existing four-year colleges and graduate institutions to make more efficient and economical use of their resources for upper-division and graduate work.
3. Offer programs of basic technical education to help meet the serious and increasing need for technical workers.
4. Provide college level programs of general education and programs of cultural activities.
5. Offer adult education programs of substance in order to meet the need for continuing education and occupational upgrading for individuals affected by a changing society.
6. Effect a positive influence on the cultural tone of the communities in the service area of the college.
7. Provide two years of college education with the greatest economy.
8. Promote better articulation between high schools and institutions of higher education.[5]

Months went by, and still the State Board of Education had not completed the study the Freeholders had petitioned. According to Dr. Guy Ferrell, the delay was caused by personnel shortages.[6] Then, on December 7, 1966, almost nine months after being petitioned by the Monmouth Freeholders, the State Department of Education finally sent its report on Monmouth County's proposed college to the Freeholders.

Although the report did not mention Monmouth College, it was, for all practical purposes, a duplication of the original 1965 Freeholders' Study Committee report. At this point, when asked if he felt it necessary to rely on Monmouth College for liberal arts and business courses in the proposed college, Mr. Irwin said, "I don't know; I wouldn't say that yet. There are arguments on both sides. It could mean a great savings by cooperating with Monmouth College, but the facilities have to be there." [7]

By January of 1967, The Red Bank Area League of Women Voters had completed a review of the Department of Education's approval to establish a county college in Monmouth County. Similar reviews were being made in the Asbury Park, Matawan, and Middletown Area Leagues. By February 2, 1967, the education chairmen from the four county Leagues had composed a press release, which expressed the following consensus:

1. There is an urgent need for a community college in Monmouth County.
2. Monmouth County is financially able to construct and operate such a college.
3. The County should aim at developing a separate multipurpose institution with its own physical plant and facilities.
4. The Board of Trustees of this institution should be qualified according to the guidelines set forth by the State Board of Education. [8]

The community's drive to establish its own multi-purpose county college appeared to gain considerable momentum at this point, with various groups and individuals stepping up their efforts to let the Freeholders and each other know where they stood on the college issue. The League of Women Voters made its position clear when a copy of the text of its press release was sent on March 17, 1967, to the Board of Chosen Freeholders. [9] The AAUW committee, with Audrie LaTowsky as spokeswoman, talked with several Freeholders. Senator Bedell recalls agreeing with AAUW and the League on the idea of independence for the proposed college: "I had established a rapport with the League of Women Voters and with the Northern Monmouth County Branch of AAUW . . . . The three of us came to the same conclusion: that we should have a college as a separate entity. . . ." [10]

Mrs. LaTowsky remembers talking frankly with Mr. Irwin at this time:

I eventually told Joe Irwin in one of our talks that we had a membership . . . maybe 450 women in AAUW . . . and we were not just talking about 450 interested women, we were talking about 450 interested women and their husbands, and their families, and the other groups where we were enlisting aid. And I said we have five little groups who are pushing for this [separate county college] and will work for this.[11]

The Freeholders were being beseiged; even the New Jersey State Department of Education clearly favored a separate institution. Earl Garrison explains that the Study Committee had talked with a number of different consultants from the State Department of Education before they finalized their plans:

They were supposedly helping us out [but] once in awhile you would get somebody from Trenton that would just *blast*—"YOU'VE GOT TO HAVE IT!" Well, that undid an awful lot that we had done before. One night we thought we were going to throw the guy [Department of Education representative] out because he turned everyone that was there against the college because he was so vehement about having it and spending the money.[12]

It appears that the constant tattoo of groups and individuals in the community had more than a little to do with a change in attitude of the Freeholders and members of their Study Committee. This change was particularly evident at the first of three public meetings on the proposed county college held by the Freeholders. These meetings, termed "cracker barrel talks" by Eugene Bedell, were prescribed by the state as a step in determining a county's need for a community college before the Freeholders would be allowed to establish such a college.

The first meeting, held at the Monmouth Shopping Center in Eatontown, New Jersey, attracted about 250 people (as estimated by the Asbury Park *Press*, April 5, 1967). According to the *Press*, only five hands were raised in response to Freeholder Danskin's asking if anyone definitely opposed the college. The League of Women Voters and the Northern Monmouth Branch of AAUW spoke in favor of a separate county college, while the Jersey Shore Branch of AAUW (which had long been closely associated with Monmouth College) spoke in favor of a county college with temporary affiliation with Monmouth College. After the meeting Freeholder Bedell stated he would support the affiliation with Monmouth College if it were guaranteed that a separate county college would open its doors within three years. Freeholder Daly, who earlier had been firmly in favor of a permanent Monmouth College affiliation, did an about face, stating that he "opposed any attempt for the county college to enter into anything but a temporary affiliation with Monmouth." [13]

Elinor Multer comments on the public meetings and the events leading up to them:

The public in general wanted a separate community college, did not want it tied in, did not want a second class . . . system. . . . During the course of those three hearings, the Freeholders began to commit themselves to the idea of a comprehensive and independent community college. To me, it was a very fascinating example of democracy in action in a way that I can't give you another example comparable. I am convinced that if it were not for the amount of public attention focused on that question [tie-in with Monmouth College] that, without a doubt, the thing would have gone through as originally envisioned with this split in the technical course being provided by the county college and the rest by Monmouth. And I think it was nothing but the arousing of the public and the not inconsiderable resulting public forum, that led to a change in that. [14]

Reports from observers at the public meetings reflect the excitement in the air and the zeal of the community groups in the audience. Carolyn Nilson, then president-elect of AAUW, recalls that AAUW spoke out "loudly for a separate institution with dignity of its own." Her responsibility was to make sure informed women from the branch study groups were in attendance at meetings held around the county. Mrs. Nilson states: "We were there, at every one of them. Throughout the public meetings . . . we spoke very loudly and with a considerable sense of urgency. . . ." [15]

Anita Bellin, who was soon to assume the position of Chairman of the Education Committee of the County Council of the League of Women Voters, recalls a memorable first meeting at Eatontown:

It coincided with an uprising of sorts on the part of the faculty of Monmouth College. There had been a major issue of academic freedom and the facts of the matter were probably pretty cloudy, with accusations on both sides. . . . People from Monmouth College attended because they felt that a free, or nearly free, public institution, would provide a greater proportion of academic freedom. . . . They truly felt that this was the forum where they would gain some public attention from the press. But that first meeting drew about 300 people, of whom . . . a good number were Monmouth College people, very angry at Monmouth College. There were probably 35 members of AAUW and 35 members of the League of Women Voters wearing signs. The ladies wore hats and buttons, and the AAUW members wore signs on their shirts identifying themselves as being members of these organizations that were in support of the independent county college . . . .

My memories of that evening . . . are so embroiled with the professors in the back of the room shouting to get the floor, and Mr. Irwin saying, "No," he wasn't going to discuss academic freedom, and the AAUW passing pieces of paper because Joe wouldn't let anyone speak more than once . . . . It was kind of all nonsense. I can distinctly remember one of the members of the League of Women Voters leaning over me and saying, "You're really not being very lady-like," and my response was, "I don't care." [16]

Whether in spite of or because of the exceptionally vocal audience, Freeholder Director Joseph C. Irwin considered the first public meeting a "very, very successful hearing," noting that there was "practically no one against the county college once they found out what it was, and how it was to be formed, and run." [1]

At the second public meeting, held in the Hall of Records, Freehold, the audience was considerably smaller and people were not restricted in the number of times they might speak. Anita Bellin recalls that Audrie LaTowsky was there with several AAUW members, and that the League of Women Voters was also represented by several people. The two groups took advantage of the unlimited speaking opportunity to filibuster. The meeting, Mrs. Bellin remembers, "went on

5.
The Turning of the Tide

in excess of two hours . . . . There were only fourteen or fif-teen of us, and we kept raising our hands. . . ."[2]

The tide, at last, began to turn when at the Freehold meet-ing Eugene Bedell and Benjamin H. Danskin indicated sup-port of the idea of an independent community college.[3] Mr. Danskin said that what finally convinced the Freeholders that they had to have a separate college was the accumulated pressure from the community. "AAUW, and everybody else was pushing for it," he said, "and I think we really explored every other angle that could have saved the county money, and finally 'bit the bullet.'"[4]

By the time of the third public meeting, the Freeholders seemed to be leaning toward locating the community college at Brookdale Farm in Middletown. Mr. Irwin explained that the third public meeting was held in Middletown because the Freeholders "had had ideas that . . . the college was going to be in the Middletown area . . . at Brookdale Farm . . ." and the Freeholders wanted to see how the officials and people of the area would react.[5]

With the changing of the Freeholders' position, Joseph C. Irwin threw himself completely behind the separate-college movement. Audrie LaTowsky reported later that she had "given him considerable credit for the fact that he did keep an open mind, and did allow himself to be won over. He was the college's most ardent supporter on the Board of Chosen Freeholders and became really 100 percent behind Brook-dale."[6]

Irwin's change of mind placed him in a particularly awk-ward position as a member of the Monmouth College Board of Trustees. With diplomatic understatement he later said,

I was the only member of the Board of Freeholders on the Monmouth College Board, and the only one close to Brookdale Community Col-lege . . . . I didn't get congratulated by the Board of Trustees at Mon-mouth College. It was a rather difficult position to be in . . . and rather embarrassing at times. But I was able to shoulder it and go on because I just felt that the two-year county [college] would help finance students —pay perhaps fifty percent of their tuition.[7]

Mr. Irwin was aware that the county college would be including occupational courses such as mechanics and electronics that Monmouth College didn't have. He came to see that "Monmouth College was a different kind of an institution entirely." In addition, Mr. Irwin stated that it would be better to separate the county college from Monmouth College because "there would be no way you could tie up a two-year community college [financed] by the Board of Freeholders to Monmouth College, because [Monmouth College] was a separate institution of its own."

(Mr. Irwin explains that before Brookdale Community College was created, the Board of Freeholders appropriated up to $100,000 a year to Monmouth College. After Brookdale opened, the Freeholders no longer gave these funds to Monmouth College, but the loss, he says, didn't affect the college greatly as that amount was less than five percent of their expenses.)[8]

More than a year later, representatives of Brookdale's Board of Trustees met with Monmouth College officials to work out an arrangement between the two institutions. Earl Garrison, who was a member of Brookdale's Board of Trustees because of his position as Superintendent of Schools in Monmouth County, recalls the final interaction:

The Board of Trustees of [Monmouth College] saw that it was inevitable that a junior college such as Brookdale was going to be formed. Dr. Van Note was on our [Freeholders' Study Committee], so knew what the situation was. I think he had some concerns about losing a portion of his students to Brookdale, but . . . I think we did do it in as smooth a way as we could.[9]

Monmouth College officials eventually agreed that until the county college set up facilities its students could earn credits at Monmouth College while receiving state and county funds to cover seventy-five percent of their tuition. The arrangement, which terminated in 1970, provided that these funds were to be paid directly to Monmouth College.

This agreement eased the resentment with which Monmouth College gave up its long, hard battle for a tie-in with the county college. Dr. Joseph I. Robinson wrote that it did something else too:

This agreement represented acknowledgment of Brookdale by Monmouth College. It also represents somewhat of a victory for Monmouth College, which by now was resigned to the community college and stood to profit well by the agreement. The effect of this agreement was that of compromise.[10]

Those who favored a separate county college also saw advantages for Monmouth College in the split. As early as 1966 Audrie LaTowsky had suggested that Monmouth College "consider dropping the lower division entirely and concentrating on the last two years and graduate school." Although the officials "were absolutely appalled by this suggestion," Mrs. LaTowsky believes that it was partially through Brookdale Community College's coming into existence that Monmouth College began its graduate program.[11]

Like Joseph Irwin, State Senator Alfred N. Beadleston, who had sponsored the original County College Bill in the state legislature, had been on Monmouth College's Board of Trustees for many years. He told interviewers, "As soon as the Monmouth County College became a reality, both Joe Irwin and I realized that you can't serve two masters—a private college and a community college—so we both got off the Board; he before I."[12] These gallant acts by two public servants of long record reflected the selflessness of Monmouth County citizens who had risen and were to rise to promote an independent county college with "a dignity of its own."

On Tuesday, July 18, 1967, the Board of Chosen Freeholders finally passed a resolution to establish an independent, two-year Monmouth County public college. By statute, forty-five days were required to pass before the resolution became law and the Freeholders could appoint a board of trustees. But the college was on its way! No one, however, dreamed that in a little more than two years Brookdale Community College would be opening its doors to students. But then no one knew that a human dynamo was to become

Brookdale's first president. That, however, is a later part of this history.

Almost immediately claims were made for the honor of being the college's founder. Freeholder Director Irwin observes wryly that Freeholders had gone through three elections talking about the institution. "They talked about the possibility of it at the first election, talked about its creation at the next, and then took credit for it in the third. . . . I was always in favor of it from the very beginning."[1]

Certainly, without the interest, good will, and resolution of the Freeholders, particularly that of Director Irwin, the college would never have been established. Without Dr. Clayton who drafted the County College Bill, without Assemblyman Beadleston who sponsored it in the legislature, without Superintendent of Schools Garrison who brought the Act to the attention of the Freeholders, and without hardworking, conscientious Freeholders like Eugene Bedell and Benjamin Danskin, there might never have been a Monmouth county college.

There were others who claimed all or part of the credit for founding the college, and since the idea of a community college had evolved from the community itself perhaps it was only to be expected that so many groups and individuals would have parental feelings toward the college. Anita Bellin voiced the opinion of many when she remarked that she was "interested in the number of people who . . . took credit for having personally promoted and personally established the college."[2] One of these people was Paul Zar, Chairman of the Citizens for Monmouth County College, who claims Brookdale as his "baby." Asked in an interview if he was pleased with the way Brookdale turned out, Zar said, "Oh, I'm excited! I'm very proud. How can a father feel to a kid?"[3]

The Northern Monmouth Branch of AAUW has always been proud to claim its share in fostering the creation of Brookdale. When the college opened its doors in October of 1969, Mary Lou Wagner, branch president at the time, wrote a congratulatory letter in behalf of the AAUW Board of

Directors to Brookdale's first president, Erwin L. Harlacher. Dr. Harlacher's reply shows his recognition for AAUW's part in founding the college:

> If it had not been for the support of the Northern Monmouth County Branch of AAUW, Brookdale Community College might very well not exist today. For your support as an organization, but even more for your support and contributions as individuals, we will be forever indebted.[4]

7.
The Ideal Location: A Triangle of Land

Fortune has smiled on Brookdale Community College in so many ways that justifiably, and without any hint of cliché, it came to be called in the 1970's "The Impossible Dream." One of the factors that helped to make the dream a reality was the acquisition of the site for the college. Benjamin Danskin, who in 1967 was Freeholder Director of Private Property, described how the inspiration for this important decision came about:

> I can still remember the conference; we [the Freeholders] came in and [were] presented this picture of [the proposed college]. Somebody said, generally to the whole conference, "Where in the world are we ever going to put it?" I said, "Excuse me a minute." I walked out of the door into my office . . . and came back with a map. I opened the map up and spread it out on the table, and I said, "That's the ideal location." It was a map of Brookdale Farm.[1]

When Mrs. Geraldine Thompson in her will left the property that is now Thompson Park to the county, Ben Danskin, along with Charles Pike, Planning Director of Monmouth County, had explored that land, as well as the large area of land next to it known as Brookdale Farm. Brookdale Farm belonged to the estate of Mrs. Thompson's son, Lewis S. Thompson, Jr. As a result of Danskin's and Pike's recommendations, the county took an option to buy Brookdale Farm, but with no specific idea that it would ever become Brookdale Community College.

The Freeholders authorized purchase of the 221-acre site for $700,000 on September 5, 1967, just four days before the death of Geraldine Livingston Thompson. It is believed that the great woman never knew of the transaction or of any plans to establish a college on the Brookdale Farm site. Money was later appropriated to the college board of trustees to buy the land from the Freeholders, at the same price, in order to assure that fifty percent of the cost would be returned to the college by the state.[2]

Although studies had been made to determine a site for the college, in the end Brookdale was selected for three reasons:

It was bigger than any other site; it was close to the Garden State Parkway and major county roads; and it was adjacent to the property that was to become Thompson Park, and the possibility of common facilities between the park and the college looked attractive.[3]

The July 18 resolution by the Freeholders to establish a college took effect at the beginning of September, 1967. At that time the Freeholders announced they would appoint the college board of trustees at their next meeting.

8.
For the
People

Anita Bellin recalls that just before that next Freeholders' meeting, Mr. Irwin discussed privately with Virginia Vreeland his suggested list of trustees. She was not pleased, nor was the League, with the fact that several of the nominees did not appear to have the qualifications that either the League or the AAUW suggested. The two groups publicly opposed not the individual people, but the composition of the list.[1]

At the next Freeholders' meeting, Mr. Irwin announced the list of proposed trustees. The roll was then called in alphabetical order for approval. It was no surprise when Eugene Bedell voted "no," but as Mrs. Bellin noted, "The surprise came when Benjamin Danskin voted 'no.'"[2] Since Freeholder Daly was in the hospital, Joseph Irwin's and Earl Garrison's "yes" votes resulted in a tie.

After a short caucus, the Freeholders announced that a revised list of the trustees would be presented soon. After this announcement the campaign was on to influence the Board of Freeholders in this decision.

As far back as June 23, 1966, the AAUW had made known its suggested qualifications for county college trustees. A letter from Mrs. LaTowsky to Director Irwin, printed in the *Daily Register* on June 30, 1966, spelled out AAUW's recommendations that an appointee should

1. Have a broad understanding of the real needs of this county community, both present and potential.
2. Be dedicated to the county college concept in New Jersey's plan for higher education for its citizens.
3. Have sufficient time and be willing to devote the necessary effort to the job.
4. Be a person of integrity and courage.
5. Have the ability to think and plan creatively.
6. Have demonstrated leadership and success either in the community or in his work.

The position of the League of Women Voters on trustee qualifications had been made known to the Freeholders in April, 1967:

One of the most important facets of the establishment of the community college is the selection of the board of trustees . . . . We feel strongly that the members of this board should be selected on the basis of their individual qualifications without regard to race, creed, color, or political affiliations.

The board of trustees of a community college should be representative of the broad spectrum of the community. There should be members from business and industry, professionals and laymen. There should be members of the world of Arts as well as the world of Science. There should be philosophers as well as economists.

While this board cannot be all things to all people, its complexion will be the determining factor in the success or failure of this institution.[3]

That first proposed list of trustees, which the Freeholders had failed to approve, was printed in the Asbury Park *Press* and the *Daily Register* on September 20, 1967:

1. Earl Garrison, County Superintendent of Schools, required by law to be one of the nine members.
2. Leon Zuckerman, Middletown, Public Relations Director, New Jersey Natural Gas Company.

3. Frank Dalton, Wall Township, Secretary of New Jersey Confederation of Bricklayers, Masons and Plasterers, and Vice-President of New Jersey state A.F.L.-C.I.O.
4. Mrs. John L. Polhemus, Neptune, past president of Monmouth County Council of Parents and Teachers.
5. Robert Edwards, President of Electronic Assistance Corporation, Red Bank.
6. Mrs. H. H. Freedman, Freehold, member of Board of Directors of MCOSS, who had served on many commissions, committees and board organizations in welfare and community service in Monmouth County.
7. David H. Means, Long Branch, Branch Manager of the New York Bank for Savings and Vice-President of the Long Branch Board of Education.
8. George Bielitz, Little Silver, President of Monmouth County National Bank.
9. Major General W. Preston Corderman (U.S. Army Ret.), Little Silver, past National President of Retired Officers.

The League of Women Voters, AAUW, and others continued to emphasize the need for qualified trustees. They found a powerful ally at this time in the press, particularly the *Daily Register*, and were gratified at the excellent coverage given their letters. The AAUW president, Carolyn Nilson, kept notes (now part of AAUW's files) recording the group's plan to bombard the press with letters regarding the necessity of a change in the list of trustees. In the space of less than a week, nine letters from AAUW members alone were printed.

On September 21, the *Daily Register* officially threw its hat in the ring for an improved list of trustees with an editorial titled "More Homework Needed." "As individuals," the piece read, "those proposed for the board are, as Mr. Irwin said, good citizens. They have fine backgrounds—and they are to be lauded for agreeing to take on such an important, time-consuming job." However, it was felt that, as a group, the appointees would not combine to give the board of trustees the versatility and the academic stature that are essential for an assignment of this type.

On September 26, another editorial in the *Register*, this

one titled "Trustee List Opposition," said that it was "good to see some opposition generating to the list of trustees proposed for the Monmouth County two-year college."

Continuing its barrage, on September 27 the *Register* ran a story, "A Matter for the Public," by Elinor Multer, saying that the public must show concern for the quality of the college's first board of trustees. Mrs. Multer stated:

A valuable member of a county college board would be the trustee who had made a careful study of the nature and characteristics of this distinctive institution. That there are such persons in Monmouth County was clearly demonstrated at the public meetings. The comments of several members of both the League of Women Voters and the Northern Monmouth County Branch of the AAUW were clearly based on study, not merely emotion. It is unfortunate that none of these women, nor any other individual with demonstrated knowledge of the community college concept is among those chosen for the Board.

On September 29, the *Register* gave front page emphasis to an article, "Restudy College List, AAUW Urges Irwin." On the same day another article, "AAUW Gives New College Staff View," was seen in the Asbury Park *Press* stating the sentiment of AAUW that "the proposed list of Trustees of the Monmouth County College should have persons from the fields of teaching or administration and the fields of arts and humanities."

A *Register* article, "League of Women Voters Council Urges Broader College Board Representation," reported on October 2 that the Monmouth County Council League of Women Voters had "expressed hope the vote by Freeholders Benjamin H. Danskin and Eugene Bedell for delay in appointing the county college board of trustees 'is a vote for a broader representation on the board.'" In the same issue, a second article headlined "County May Alter College Board List," gave the first hint that a new list might be forthcoming.

The importance of the *Register*'s drive to influence the Freeholders to produce an improved list of trustees cannot be underestimated. *Daily Register* editor Arthur Z. Kamin says that he considers the *Daily Register*'s part in helping to get a revised list of trustees the paper's major contribution "to getting the college under way because . . . the first board chose the first president and set the character of the college as far as the construction and general overall approach of the college."[4]

Audrie LaTowsky recalls that "there were other groups that were not happy [with the first list of trustees]."[5]

In addition to writing letters, AAUW members also made phone calls and visits to the Freeholders, even meeting with Joseph C. Irwin at his home in Red Bank. Looking back on that meeting on September 25, 1967, Carolyn Nilson says, "It was a very good meeting. Irwin was very attentive. He was willing to hear us out and he asked us what our concerns were, and we expressed those concerns to him. . . . He heard us and listened to us and soon came out with a different list." Mrs. Nilson recalls that at no time during that meeting was mention made of having an AAUW member on the board of trustees. "We were just saying that we wanted good people who we felt would have the proper vision for this kind of institution."[6]

On October 3, the *Register* reported that the Freeholders had unanimously approved a new list of trustees for the county college. Four changes had been made: Added to the list were Marvin Clark, Freehold, County Agricultural Agent; Audrie LaTowsky, New Shrewsbury, Chairman of the AAUW County College Study Committee; James R. Greene, Fair Haven, Vice-President of the International Division of Manufacturers Hanover Trust Co., New York; and William O. Fleckenstein, Rumson, Executive Director of the Data and PBX Divisions at Bell Telephone Laboratories, Holmdel. Removed from the list were Frank Dalton, Robert Edwards, Mrs. H. H. Freedman and George Bielitz (who could not serve because of business reasons).

The selection of Mrs. LaTowsky seems to have been a major factor in bringing community groups to accept the final list of trustees. Although the AAUW branch had never officially put forth Mrs. LaTowsky's name as a potential trustee, Carolyn Nilson remembers personally suggesting "Audrie's name to Joe Irwin . . . . Audrie was a good choice . . . because she was knowledgeable, and with all of us behind her he was fairly assured of at least some constituency to back up his decision."[7]

Anita Bellin says that the League was "strongly pushing that some members of either the League or AAUW ought to be on that board because without the combined efforts of the two groups, there probably never would have been a Brookdale Community College."[8]

Eugene Bedell relates that when the final list of trustees was being considered, he was told by the Freeholders he would have one appointee on this board. His choice was Audrie LaTowsky. He "didn't know she was a Republican," but said, "it wouldn't have made any difference anyway."[9] Benjamin Danskin states: "She was named because she came right out of that group [AAUW]. . . . She checked out every way, even to the bonus of having been a great Republican."[10]

Mrs. LaTowsky herself, however, says that as late as the September 25, 1967, meeting of the AAUW leaders with Mr. Irwin, she had "absolutely no idea of serving on that board. It did not enter my mind."[11] She was to serve almost six years on Brookdale's Board of Trustees, nearly five of them as Vice-Chairman.

Former Freeholder Director Irwin now looks back on those days when names of proposed trustees were flying thick and fast. The Freeholders, he says,

. . . just got together and agreed and disagreed. And we fought it out among ourselves and finally came up with a satisfactory number of people, individual people that would satisfy everybody. So, in the final analysis there was no disagreement on the Board [of Freeholders] whatsoever with the final group that we appointed.[12]

The Freeholders and Mr. Irwin were praised for the new list of nominees. An October 4 editorial in the *Register* pointed out that "It was not easy for the Freeholders—especially Director Joseph C. Irwin—to make changes in the initial group of nominees," but that "fortunately, Mr. Irwin knows the meaning of the word statesmanship—and he reacted to the pleas of this newspaper and citizens throughout the county who wanted a more well-rounded, versatile board of trustees."

As the new college took shape and finally emerged as one of the most highly respected county colleges in the state, the Freeholders were to be thanked again by those who knew of other county colleges whose freeholders had *not* granted complete autonomy to their college boards of trustees. Former Freeholder Director Irwin explains how the autonomy of Brookdale's Board of Trustees came about:

It was my intent that once they were appointed . . . politics shouldn't enter into the damn thing at all . . . it's two different categories entirely . . . . Why should a bunch of elected Freeholders start telling them how to run a college? That's the worst thing in the world. . . . Once we appointed the board of trustees we said, "Look, it is your responsibility."[13]

And so it happened that Brookdale Community College began, grew, and prospered without any member of its board of trustees ever leaving a board meeting to check with a politician on how he should vote.

Through the years, as the people of Monmouth County gave freely of their time, energy, and talents to create Brookdale Community College, so the college today returns its gifts to the community a hundred, even a thousand fold.

Geraldine Thompson would be pleased.

PART III:
BROOKDALE COMMUNITY COLLEGE

Section II:
The Impossible Dream by Nancy Swann

It is April, 1969, and you have only until September to remodel two century-old horse barns into an academic complex. Your first job is to get forty horses out of the barns, and the trainer refuses to move them. At last you find a new home for the horses, renovate the barns into two stunning buildings, and open the campus for classes on schedule. Then you discover that the flies refuse to believe that the horses have left.

The usual problems faced by administrators founding a college? Hardly. But then "usual" is the last word anyone would think of applying to Brookdale Community College. Who ever heard of a corncrib as a campus monument? A "college without walls"? The whole population of a county as its student body?

For that matter, imagine a college Vietnam War rally that ended with the left and right's pledging to respect each other's opinions and uniting to keep the college functioning. But Geraldine Thompson, mistress of Brookdale Farm, had always marched to a different drummer. She would not have wanted a run-of-the-mill college, indistinguishable from hundreds of others, to bear the name of her farm. She cared about individuals—from Presidents to stable boys—and she respected their differences. That is what Brookdale Community College is all about.

When the newly-appointed board of trustees was holding its first meetings in late 1967, Earl Garrison estimated that the college could be operational in a minimum of three years and "certainly" in five years.[1] Those were the days when everyone was humming "The Impossible Dream," but no one foresaw that this particular dream would become a working reality in less than two years.

At the first meeting of the trustees on October 11, 1967, four Freeholders—Joseph C. Irwin, Eugene Bedell, Benjamin Danskin, and Harry Larrison—were present. Mr. Irwin clarified the option the Freeholders had on 221 acres of land on Newman Springs and Phalanx Roads in Lincroft. They left it up to the trustees whether to purchase the land for the new county college.

An even more pressing need was to formulate a budget and submit it before November 15 to the State Board of Higher Education for inclusion in the 1969 state budget. Approval would assure state reimbursement of half the cost, or up to $600, for each student and payment by the state of half the construction costs. The trustees appointed Earl Garrison their temporary chairman and authorized him to ask the State Board to review the Lincroft property for possible purchase.

By the second meeting, on October 18, the trustees had drawn up a budget and had decided to purchase the 221-acre Thompson estate. According to General W. Preston Corderman, the trustees were as delighted with the site as the Freeholders had been. "We were so pleased with it that we said 'Great! We would like it!'" he recalls.[2]

For many members of the Board, the property's central location and accessibility by highway and public transit—crucial for a commuting student body—weighed heavily. It was close to the Garden State Parkway and Route 34 and convenient to north-south public transportation.[3] Earl Garrison pointed out that "natural science programs would be much better because of [Thompson] Park's being adjacent to it, and there are some common facilities that could be used."[4]

According to Trustee Marvin Clark, the decision of the trustees to buy the land, subject to state approval, was unanimous.[5] "We didn't go out and look much further, because it was ideal," declared Leon Zuckerman.[6] So the property was purchased for $700,000.

Agreement on all decisions would be too much to ask, but Trustee William Fleckenstein was struck repeatedly in the early days by how well everyone worked together:

I suppose the most impressive thing I can say . . . is that it turned out to be a marvelous group of people that served on the board. . . . I believe that it is the nicest group of people I have had the occasion to work with in any community service I have ever been engaged in. So that did make it very easy to get a lot done in the early days very quickly.[7]

This rapport has continued and is largely responsible for

the astonishing rate at which Brookdale has developed and progressed over the years.

The college now had a campus; it needed a name and a president. The board of trustees appointed Audrie LaTowsky, General Corderman, Leon Zuckerman, and Earl Garrison to develop standards for the selection of a president and to screen candidates.

The need to start building on the campus, as well as the need for an interim program to provide post-high school education for at least some county residents before the college opened its doors, made long-range financial planning necessary. Therefore, on November 13, 1967, the trustees adopted a $9.3 million budget, with about $1.1 million earmarked for current expenses and $8.2 million set aside for capital expenditures over a period of five years.

The capital outlay was for the first phase of the building program, and current expenses would include tuition for about 700 county college students at Monmouth College, a private college in West Long Branch.

The board also elected General Corderman its permanent chairman, with William Fleckenstein as vice-chairman. The name "Monmouth County Community College" was adopted for the fledgling institution. The name was later changed, of course, but Leon Zuckerman felt it was important that the word "community" be there from the start, "because we felt right from the inception that we should be community oriented."[8]

The search for a president was on. With his usual wit, Trustee Marvin Clark recalls the criteria for selection: "You had to be a genius, you had to be able to get along with people, you had to have experience in administration, you had to have experience in education, and you had to be all sorts of things."[9] It was a tall order, and it took four months of intensive advertising, screening, and interviewing to fill.

The problem of educating students under the auspices of Monmouth College for the next few years was more readily solved. Monmouth College contracted to educate a certain number of students enrolled in the county college for the

1968-69 academic year, with the state and county paying the difference between the community college's tuition and Monmouth's usual rate. However, county college freshmen would have to meet the private institution's admission standards and take its usual freshman curriculum alongside private students. Only about 600 students could be accommodated under the plan.

By then, the search committee had scrutinized the credentials of fifty-six candidates for the presidency. All but six were eliminated, and in January, 1968, the remaining contenders were interviewed in person by the full board of trustees. Among the six was Dr. Ervin L. Harlacher, the thirty-eight-year-old Executive Vice-President of Oakland Community College in Bloomfield Hills, Michigan. He had not applied for the job. Dr. Harlacher recalls:

> The trustees' search committee contacted me, and it was kind of a bolt from the blue when I got the call at Oakland. . . . [Leon Zuckerman] wondered if it would be possible for me to come to Monmouth County to meet with a search committee . . . during the holidays. I said that by coincidence we were coming to New York for New Years. . . . And we had lunch at the Shadowbrook with Leon and members of the search committee. The interesting thing is that my wife and son were with me and participated in the luncheon.[10]

On the basis of the luncheon, at which Dr. Harlacher recalled "we certainly did get into what a comprehensive community college was," [11] he was invited for a meeting a week later with the entire board.

To this day, Ervin Harlacher does not know definitely who recommended him for the presidency although he has always assumed it was Dr. Lamar Johnson, his major professor at U.C.L.A.[12] His uncertainty is not surprising, for Leon Zuckerman says that the committee received his name from more than one source. "U.C.L.A. and two or three others sent us his name and the write-up they had on him," says Zuckerman. "We pursued it from there." [13] Audrie LaTowsky recalls that one of the recommendations came from former Harlacher associate Cal Flint, of Foothills College in California.[14]

Coming as he did from Oakland, a community college with a novel educational program, Ervin Harlacher was bound to have bold new ideas of what a community college should be. Oakland's method was based on heavy use of nonprint media and computerization of learning. Dr. Harlacher did not agree with all that was being done at Oakland, but he had innovative ideas that appealed to most of the trustees. Audrie LaTowsky says that "he was able to put into words the things that some of us felt should happen."[15]

General Corderman echoes her reaction:

He was dynamic. He had ideas that appealed to us in the way of having . . . a county college be a truly community college and to reach out and serve the county. . . . A community college . . . serves not only the student but the community in which it was established. And this, Dr. Harlacher believed, is what a community college should do.[16]

Dr. Harlacher and the board found that they agreed on another key point: that Monmouth County Community College should offer not only the first two years of the traditional college program, but also be strong in vocational and technical programs.

Ervin Harlacher was completely frank about the fact that, if he were named president, the college would have to adopt his philosophy. But his philosophy seemed to fit that of most of the trustees the way the right key fits a lock. It was a combination that would open the door to educational, vocational, and cultural opportunity for thousands of Monmouth County residents.

The trustees and Dr. Harlacher agreed that the door should be wide open. Mrs. LaTowsky explains, "We felt strongly that it be an open door institution, meaning that everyone who wished to enter Brookdale could get into Brookdale. . . . You can have an open door, but it is not a revolving door."[17]

Ervin Harlacher explains what this idea means:

I emphasized my belief in mastery learning. . . . That a student should not be able to go through a community college and receive an Associate degree who can't read at a certain level . . . write at a certain level . . .

do math at a certain level. The concept . . . of keeping the door open but . . . assuring that those who go out the other end with credentials can indeed perform. . . . I also discussed my belief in extensive community services of a non-credit nature. . . . [18]

Unlike most other applicants, Dr. Harlacher was not then the president of a community college. But everywhere the trustees inquired about him they received outstanding recommendations. The most influential was that of Dr. Lamar Johnson of U.C.L.A., one of the country's leaders in community college education. "He told us that if we could get [Harlacher] at any price, he would be the best man we could get," [19] Leon Zuckerman said.

Dr. Ervin L. Harlacher, founding president of Brookdale Community College.

A month after the interview, General Corderman called Dr. Harlacher and told him that he was the unanimous choice of the board. After careful consideration, he accepted.

Interestingly, the salary offered was slightly less than he had been receiving at Oakland. Moreover, soon after Dr. Harlacher accepted Brookdale's offer, the president of Oakland resigned, and Dr. Harlacher took over as acting president there. Why, then, did he come to Monmouth County? Dr. Harlacher does not say, but Mrs. LaTowsky surmises, "I really feel he made his choice because he felt he would have a chance at Brookdale to start right on the ground floor and build a community college."[20]

Dr. Harlacher's task of simultaneously running Oakland and engaging in the groundwork needed to get Brookdale under way involved considerable physical inconvenience: "I had to extend my stay in Oakland until the first of July. . . . I went back and forth in the meantime, spending a couple of days in Monmouth County and the rest of the time in Oakland County."[21]

Two-year public community colleges had been in existence in the West—especially in California—for many years, but they represented a concept unfamiliar to most New Jersey residents. People who had heard of them at all generally assumed that they were cut-down versions of a four-year college. This misconception alone would have made extensive public re-education necessary. Added to it were Dr. Harlacher's commitment to highly innovative educational techniques and his commitment—enthusiastically shared by the trustees —to community services, as outlined in his book, *The Community Dimension of the Community College* (1968). It became clear that an intensive public relations campaign, through press releases and personal appearances by Dr. Harlacher and the trustees, would be needed to bring the message of the community college to the people it would serve.

Although burdened by a grueling commuting schedule, the new president lost no time in explaining the Brookdale concept to Monmouth County residents. He was admirably suited to the task, having received a Master's degree in Journalism before earning his D.Ed. degree. On March 2, 1968, he introduced what was to be his favorite theme: Monmouth County Community College would have the whole county as its campus and the total population as its student body.

Dr. Harlacher also spelled out five fundamental purposes the new community college would serve. He asserted that the new college would

—Admit all high school graduates and others over the age of nineteen who can profit from instruction.

—Permit the country's qualified youth and adults to complete the first two years of college at home at nominal costs.

—Provide occupational training programs for those who intend to enter gainful employment at the end of two years of college or less.

—Be an educational resource center for all of Monmouth County.

—Provide flexible programs of learning ... tailored to meet individual needs, and which employ in a systematic way all of the human resources and technological developments available to the college.[22]

On that same date, March 2, 1968, Dr. Harlacher proposed to the trustees that, instead of merely doing the difficult in three to five years, the new college should do the impossible in two years—open on its own campus in the fall of 1969! He was not sure whether temporary quarters would be needed or whether it would be feasible to remodel the sturdy old barns still standing on the property. The trustees doubted that it would be done, but they were willing to try to meet Dr. Harlacher's target date.

What prompted their decision? A major factor was that the arrangement with Monmouth College was far from adequate. The private college had already rejected several applicants, and disappointed parents and students were complaining. In addition, the 650 Brookdale freshmen Monmouth College could accommodate were a mere handful compared to the number of people desiring low-cost, post-high school education.

By April of 1968, Monmouth College had rejected 148 out

of 963 applicants, and Dr. Harlacher's proposal seemed to make more and more sense. At their April 2 meeting, the trustees authorized renovation by May 15 of a small house on the Brookdale Farm property for use as a college office. The college was off the drawing board!

That same evening, the trustees hired Mrs. Edith Reilly as secretary to the president. Since Dr. Harlacher was still at Oakland much of the time, Mrs. Reilly became the first employee of the new college. Still with her beloved Brookdale as Secretary to the Board of Trustees, Mrs. Reilly is known by all as "the first lady of Brookdale."

The small house on Newman Springs Road where the College began.

Edith Reilly's association with Ervin Harlacher did not begin at Brookdale but at Oakland, where she was a secretary. When Dr. Harlacher learned that the Reillys were planning to return to their native New Jersey, he offered Edith a job as his secretary at Brookdale. She was delighted to accept. "You don't often get the opportunity to be the first employee of a college that hasn't been built yet," she declares proudly.[23]

In early April the trustees visited Oakland to see some of Ervin Harlacher's ideas in operation, although the Oakland program was not in complete accord with his concepts. He found the use of many media in education exciting, but he seems to have found the heavily computerized instruction at Oakland more than a bit chilly. In light of the intimate student-faculty rapport he fostered at Brookdale, one cannot imagine Dr. Harlacher's agreeing with an unnamed Oakland official who said, "Facts . . . are transmitted by a machine just as well as by the teacher. The teacher is the extension of the machine."[24]

General Corderman found the trip valuable: "If he went ahead with that philosophy, even though we agreed . . . we would have reservations if we . . . weren't fully convinced before the buildings were built."[25] It was crucial for everyone to agree on educational principles before the construction began, because central to the implementation of Ervin Harlacher's educational concepts was open-space construction—learning areas separated only by low partitions—rather than enclosed classrooms. The other trustees were also favorably impressed by what they saw at Oakland. (To this day, William Fleckenstein has fond memories of the Beef Wellington that Food Services students prepared and served them!)[26]

Dr. Harlacher intended to adapt Oakland's "learner-centered instructional systems" approach for use at Brookdale. Brookdale student Joseph King described this approach in the Woodbridge *News-Tribune*:

> The learning objectives . . . are spelled out at the start of the course. The work is programmed in units, and the student can work at his or her own pace.
>
> There is one large assembly and several small seminar-type sessions per week. . . . The learner-centered approach makes extensive use of learning laboratories where the student can find course material in books, programmed texts, film strips, tape decks, and movies.[27]

Elinor Ebeling, a librarian and media specialist who is now Dean of the Learning Resources Center at Brookdale, joined the staff in August, 1969. She was attracted to her job by the way the college's Learning Resources Center, or library, would interfile books and non-print media together in one card catalogue to permit the student to learn in his or her own way: "It was appealing to let the student learn at any level. If they were not readers, but could listen to tapes, they could learn this way. If they were more visual, they could learn through the visual things you could have available."[28] For the readers, of course, there were books—some 13,000 volumes when the college opened.

Dr. Harlacher, in the meantime, was accepting speaking engagements around Monmouth County to bring Brookdale's message to the people. He emphasized his favorite refrains of the whole county as a campus and all county residents as the student body. He made it clear that in addition to credit programs, academic and vocational, Brookdale would come into its own through community-service-oriented education.

In June, 1968, the trustees approved the appointment of two more former associates of Dr. Harlacher at Oakland. Thomas H. Auch, Director of Business and Finance at Oakland, was hired as Brookdale's Dean of Administrative Services. Merrill G. Miller, Dr. Harlacher's assistant at Oakland, became Assistant to the President at Brookdale. Later, some members of the Oakland faculty joined the teaching staff.

Ervin and Norma Jo Harlacher and their son Mark moved into their new home in Shrewsbury in early July and became aware of a new problem: Even in those early days, people were confusing Monmouth College and Monmouth County Community College. It was certain that Monmouth College would not go shopping for another name, so the staff of the county college resolved to find a new name for their institution. The trustees and administrators considered several alternatives, but what name could be more fitting than "Brookdale," in honor of Brookdale Farm? Therefore, on July 8, 1969, the trustees officially renamed the school "Brookdale Community College, the County College of Monmouth."

The newspapers hailed the name change, not only because it would end the confusion between the two colleges, but also because, as the Asbury Park *Press* put it, "Brookdale will perpetuate the name of its one-time owner, the Thompson family, one of which, Mrs. Geraldine Thompson, was distinguished in the field of philanthropy and a leading citizen of Monmouth County."[29]

The Freeholders, on the other hand, were not so enthusiastic. They wanted "Monmouth County" in the name. Freeholder Ben Danskin, always a man to speak his mind, was distressed: "Here we had this Monmouth County Community College being built. We wanted it to be a showcase . . . and we didn't want any mistake that it wasn't the Monmouth County college. We felt most strongly—I was particularly vocal on that. I didn't like the change."[30] But the Freeholders did not try to impose their views, nor did they expect to be allowed to.

Finances are still the only area in which the Freeholders exercise control over the trustees. As Ben Danskin puts it, "We get input at budget time. This is where they had to come in and 'dance the tune.' They had to come in and convince us every year that what they wanted to do the following year was correct. They did! That's the hold the board [of Freeholders] should have on them."[31]

"Dancing the tune" at budget time has always been Thomas Auch's task, and he prefers to do the job armed with flip charts. He calls it "looking for money with charts and graphs. . . . I've been ridiculed often because I like to use flip charts. I just sometimes think that a well-constructed flip chart can explain everything very simply."[32]

No one remembers exactly when Dr. Harlacher first dubbed Brookdale "The Impossible Dream," but Mr. Auch said it was very soon after the Harlachers arrived. The hit song from "Man of La Mancha," the Broadway musical based on the story of Don Quixote, had captured the imagination of the nation. Americans with unfulfilled aspirations identified with the old Spanish knight's determination to right unrightable wrongs, defeat unbeatable foes, and "reach the unreachable star." With all the obstacles that had to be hurdled in starting Brookdale, a natural process of association made "The Impossible Dream" Ervin Harlacher's theme song. "It . . . followed him through the college," Mr. Auch said.[33]

Opening a new college a full two years ahead of schedule did seem impossible. How was it done? By careful planning, good luck (in the form of two fine old horse barns), imagination, and hard, round-the-clock work by the president, the trustees, and the staff. Behind it all was the driving force of Dr. Harlacher's total determination that they were going to do it.

Thomas Auch recalls,

Erv had a concept that absolutely nothing was impossible. I would have accepted that we couldn't open in 1969, probably. . . . One of the things that makes presidents is their absolute determination and their unwillingness to compromise. Erv had a concept that Brookdale should open in September of '69, and there was no retreating from that position.[34]

Dr. Harlacher's determination was buttressed by the spirit of cooperation among the members of the board of trustees.

To accomplish its impossible goal, Brookdale needed a master plan. Dr. Harlacher and the trustees decided that hiring professional planning consultants would be the most efficient and economical way of acquiring one. Accordingly, on August 1, 1969, the trustees approved a $163,690 contract with General Learning Corporation, an educational planning affiliate of Time-Life, Inc.

The Master Plan that GLC agreed to provide included a survey of the community, curriculum determinations, enrollment projections, a feasibility study for an interim campus, development of educational specifications as a guide to campus construction, and a site development study. At no additional cost, GLC would perform computer simulation of college operations for ten years, allowing cost comparison of alternate curricula and teaching methods.

The survey of the community was to determine the educational and occupational needs of Brookdale's 500-square-mile campus, Monmouth County. It would serve as a guide for establishing career training programs.

The educational specifications were needed as a guide to the building of permanent college facilities, so that the architects could develop building layouts and divisions of interior space that would best implement Brookdale's course offerings, teaching methods, and services. "Brookdale was to be built around the program," Audrie LaTowsky emphasized, "not the program around Brookdale. The physical plant itself was built to house the program."[35]

This last feature of the plan resulted in a financial saving that more than paid for the whole GLC contract. Leon Zuckerman explained, "Through the use of some of the actual physical planning of the campus [by GLC] . . . when we finally decided on architects we were able to negotiate their fees downward . . . because much of the work had been done in this Master Plan. So that [considering] the money that we actually spent on the Master Plan, we saved much more than that in the reduction of the fees to the architects."[36]

Over the next couple of months, GLC sent the trustees, in groups in two or three, to operating community colleges throughout the country to see what was being done elsewhere. General Corderman recalls, "We went to Chicago, we went to Missouri, we went to Maryland. . . . It was a training period. . . . It eliminated the possibility of reservations when we agreed to things, and I think it was probably an extremely valuable step in our development of what is now Brookdale Community College."[37]

The trustees saw many things they wanted to have at Brookdale, and also many things they emphatically did *not* want. Marvin Clark recalls sourly the head of an audio-visual department who had stacks of unused equipment. And there was the Food Services teacher in Nevada, formerly a famous chef on the Las Vegas Strip, who insisted on preparing everything himself while the students watched disconsolately. "They didn't even have the opportunity to make a mistake!" Clark complained.[38]

In mid-May, 1968, the college had opened a center of operation in the little, white brick-and-frame house (now the college Police Station), and now Brookdale acquired an address: 765 Newman Springs Road, Lincroft. The setup was rough-and-ready at first. Yet this period had a distinct *élan* born of the staff's good-humored resourcefulness. Because there was no room elsewhere for it, the duplicating machine sat in the kitchen, next to the appliances. There were no desks, so everyone made do with card tables or furniture left by the previous occupants. Edith Reilly was the first staff member to go to work in the little house, and she has vivid memories of her time there:

We had no furniture, no equipment. We had to start from scratch. I had a card table and a folding chair, a typewriter and a telephone. [Dr. Harlacher] had a small table I think they found in the basement. . . . I was first in the office all by myself. Dr. Harlacher was still in Michigan. He would come in maybe one day a week. . . . We did all our work over the telephone.[39]

Three bedrooms and a sitting room on the second floor became office space for Merrill Miller, Thomas Auch, and his new assistant, Shirley Zeisel, and their secretaries.

In July—shortly after the Harlachers moved to New Jersey—some office furniture, including a much-needed desk for Mrs. Reilly, was added.

Mrs. Zeisel, who is now Secretary of the Colts Neck Township Board of Education, will never forget her first day on the job, in mid-July: "I came to work on a Monday morning and drove up behind the building at 8:30. . . . Edith was outside crying. . . . She told me the building had been broken into the night before. . . . They had broken her new desk and had just done a lot of unpleasant things."[40]

Aside from this episode, Mrs. Reilly has only happy memories of those days in the little brick house:

In the early days, the exciting days, when we started working in the house, we were a small family, and the house was fixed up very nicely. And we would have people coming in and inquiring about the college . . . and we would have a map that we could show them. A lot of the time people were driven around just to show them the property. . . . We worked long, hard hours. But it was very rewarding. It was just like a dream, when we look out at the campus today. . . . Many, many times we had box lunches brought in for dinner and stayed until eleven or twelve o'clock at night going over plans for the college. It was great fun.[41]

General Corderman observed that the liberal arts program, providing the first two years of college for students who wanted to transfer to four-year colleges, was fairly standard at all county colleges. The career programs, on the other hand, needed to be geared to the occupational needs of Monmouth County. To supplement the GLC survey, Dr. Harlacher asked for advice from the community, in particular from people who could advise him on establishing courses to train students to fill available jobs in Monmouth County.[42] By the end of December, an official advisory board called Brookdale Citizens was established.

In September, 1968, Mrs. Elinor Multer, an education writer for the *Daily Register*, was hired as Public Information Coordinator for the college. "I was the fourth member of the staff," she stated. "It is very rare that a community college picks its public relations person at that stage of the game."[43] Her appointment, as Dr. Harlacher pointed out, was needed because "while there is great public interest in the college, there is also a lack of information about its goals."[44]

When the staff eventually had to expand into another small house near the white brick one, Shirley Zeisel literally "grabbed her hammer and nails," rounded up carpenters, plumbers, and electricians, and outfitted the house as a business office.[45]

No one is sure just when it occurred to Dr. Harlacher and the trustees to make the buildings on the farm, especially those two enormous, sturdy horse barns, into permanent campus buildings. However, Mrs. LaTowsky recalls that she "just fell in love with those barns" the very first time she went out to look at the land:

The first comment I made was that surely we can find some use for those barns. Joe Irwin . . . said, "By the time you spend money converting something like that you might as well knock them down and start all over again." I said I just thought it was a tragedy, that this was part of history . . . and that we could use them. Of course, when Erv Harlacher saw them, immediately his great vision came forth. And this was when we thought we could convert them into buildings and use them to get Brookdale started, much sooner than if we had to have the whole facility built. And we had building engineers come in to determine the structural strength of those buildings. They said that indeed they were in excellent condition. . . .[46]

The more they all thought about the idea the better they liked it. Dr. Harlacher was deeply committed to the use of open-space construction. Except for the low partitions of the horse stalls, the barns were almost pure open space. They were, in Ervin Harlacher's words, "modern open space modules." GLC had also recommended accelerating on-campus development by using existing structures.

The trustees and staff considered architectural firms from all over the country, and whether or not an architect wanted to keep the barns became a very effective screening standard. Elinor Multer recalled "one New Jersey friend that I think expected to go away with the contract. . . . He was not on the premises ten minutes when he said, 'Well, we'll tear these down.' He never came back; that was the end of that."[47]

Architects Bernard Kellenyi of Red Bank and John Shaver of Salina, Kansas, shared great enthusiasm for the barns and the exciting possibilities they offered. Naturally there are other qualifications for building a college than a fondness for old barns, and Shaver and Kellenyi had these qualities in abundance. They were formally hired on December 16, 1968.

Leon Zuckerman felt that Shaver had an excellent grasp of the relationship between "the human elements, the academic elements, and the physical elements"[48] in planning the many open-space schools he had designed in Kansas.

Ervin Harlacher has observed that "the open-space school to a very great extent is a return to the one-room school house, with a certain amount of modern technology added and a recognition that bright students can do a great deal on their own."[49] Leon Zuckerman saw this idea in action when, with four other trustees, he went out to Kansas to see school buildings Shaver had designed. He came home completely sold:

John Shaver took us to one school with open-space . . . an elementary school that had one big room . . . no interior walls. And in the four corners there were four classrooms. In one area the teacher was sitting on the floor with the children. Another area, they had some seats there. The teacher was talking to them. And we walked through . . . all together, ten or so adults. And the most remarkable thing, here were these kids out in the open, and none of them really looked up or were distracted by us. . . . I turned to the principal of the school and I said to him, "Don't you find that this kind of atmosphere is very disruptive and distracting to the kids?" "Well," he said, "you have been standing here talking with us for five minutes. Have you seen any of them turn around and look?"[50]

Bernard Kellenyi was a well-known Red Bank architect with an excellent reputation and knowledge of local contractors and building materials. Kellenyi had one additional qualification that was to prove indispensable: he had already turned a barn into a school building. He had done Christian Brothers Academy: "They started with a barn. . . . They had the property . . . and they wanted to open up quickly. And we had converted the barn."[51] The Shaver-Kellenyi partnership seemed perfect.

The Freeholders made no public comment on the decision to renovate the barns. They were not going to interfere, but the general tone of their private reactions was captured by Benjamin Danskin:

When they came back and said, "We're going to use the barns," I said, "You're out of your mind! You can't do it! Put a bulldozer in and get rid of them—no way!" I can remember being very, very vocal about the fact that the architect had suddenly lost his mind. I said I don't object to setting the farm tempo—I loved that—but to use those barns! Kellenyi had to go to great lengths to prove to us that not only could he use the barns but he could use them within the framework of financial responsibility.[52]

In fact, using the barns saved both time and money. The renovating cost only half what new construction would have.

Weather made work impossible until spring. The architects needed time to draw up their plans. And—not an insignifi-

Architects from Bernard Kellenyi group in Red Bank look over what is now the Creative Arts Center.

cant consideration—there were forty horses still living in the barns!

2.
Turning
Point

The January, 1969, meeting of the board of trustees was crucial. Before anything could be done, a budget providing the funds had to be passed. The meeting was covered for the Newark *Evening News* by Linda Ellis (now a reporter for the *Daily Register*), who re-creates that dramatic evening:

We sat at student desks at the elementary school in Lincroft. Reporters from the *Daily Register*, the Asbury Park *Press*, the *News-Tribune* and I, representing the Newark *Evening News*, were busily taking notes as, on that night of January 20, 1969, Ervin L. Harlacher met with the full board for the first time since he had been installed as president of the fledgling Brookdale Community College.

The barns were then vast, deserted structures. Those same barns in years to come were to earn national recognition for architects Bernard Kellenyi of Red Bank and John Shaver of Salina, Kansas, who planned and supervised their restoration.

But before barn renovation, before the school could purchase so much as a single textbook, the budget had to be approved by the Board of Chosen Freeholders.

Much of the time that early meeting was given over to discussion of how to present a bare-bones budget that would not get tangled in Trenton—or in Freehold.

Trustees and Dr. Harlacher discussed income first. It made the outgo sound less frightening.

The tuition that would come in from the approximately 1,000 students who would enter in the fall of 1969 had been set by the Freeholders. Tuition for full-time students (carrying 12 or more credits) was tabbed at $150 per session for Monmouth County residents.

Today, the college's 1977-78 budget, introduced in February, 1977, calls for $250 per session for those living in the county. The state and county have always paid the costs that tuition did not cover. In 1969, the total cost per student was about $1,350.

Back in 1969, New Jersey residents from outside the county would pay $375 per session, and out-of-state students were to be billed $675. These costs have increased at approximately the same rate as the tuition for Monmouth County residents.

Part-time students were to be charged $12.50 per credit hour. Out-of-county students would pay $31.75 and out-of-state, $56.25 per credit hour. (For 1977-78, the cost per credit hour is $18.75.)

In exchange for that money, Brookdale officials had to provide curricula acceptable to the county and state. At that time, the first month of 1969, the program of study had only preliminary approval from the Brookdale trustees. It had yet to go to the State Board of Higher Education for acceptance.

The night of the meeting in early 1969, the trustees received a seemingly routine approval. The State Board of Higher Education gave the nod to a plan to renovate the stables on the Brookdale campus for September classroom use. Afterward, as a result of this approval, came the magnificent restoration of the main barns, work that was featured in a national magazine and numerous architectural trade journals.

Near the close of the meeting, Dr. Harlacher went through the curricula course by course.

"I hope, in time," he said prophetically, "we can add courses in law enforcement, social work, and recreation."

They did.

State approval of the barn renovations and Freeholder approval of the budget meant that the impossible dream was on its way to realization. Dr. Harlacher committeed Brookdale to providing educational facilities for 1,000 full-time students and an equal number of part-time students by fall of 1969, through use of the remodeled barns and rented space in such facilities as schools and churches throughout the county. Another valuable resource was added formally on February 14, 1969, when the Monmouth County Vocational Board of Education transferred ownership of the Monmouth County Technical Institute to Brookdale. The Institute, located on the former NIKE missile base in Middletown, provided post-high-school vocational and technical education to county residents. The Vocational Board felt that these post-high-school studies could be administered more efficiently by the new county college. The base gave the staff additional space in which to work while campus renovations proceeded, and it also provided expensive technical equipment needed for many of the college's career training programs.

Donald P. Hoagland, Superintendent of the County Vocational School District, observes that turning the institute over to the college has avoided the costly and wasteful situation existing in other New Jersey counties, with county college and the vocational school boards competing for funds for virtually identical programs.[1]

Because of space limitations, it was possible that all applicants might not be accommodated initially; it was therefore necessary to develop an admissions policy. This task fell to Fred B. Hazlett, appointed in January of 1969 as Brookdale's Director of Admissions, a post he had held previously at Middlesex County College. "My assignment was to put together an admissions program from the ground up," he said. "Admissions procedures, regulations, forms, office procedures, the whole business."[2]

GLC's survey and the feedback from Brookdale Citizens paid off: the curricula that Harlacher presented and had approved at the January meeting of the Board were comprehensive and solidly rooted in the needs of the community.

3.
The College Without Walls

A view of the first and second floors of Barn A when the building opened.

The transfer programs to be offered were Business, Education, Engineering, Humanities, Mathematics, Science, and Social Science.

The career education programs were in three categories. The first, Allied Health Programs, included Inhalation Therapy, Medical Laboratory Technology, Nursing, and Radiologic Technology. These were to depend heavily on hospital facilities in the county.

The second set of career programs included Accounting, Business Administration, Computer Science, Retailing and

Marketing, and Secretarial Science.

The third category, Engineering Technology, would encompass Automotive Technology, Drafting and Design, Electronics, and Instrumentation. These, along with the academic transfer Science programs, would be offered at the NIKE base.

By this time, along with "the whole county is our campus," Brookdale had another motto: "the college without walls." Of course there would be no interior walls (except in spaces designed for large lecture sessions) in the campus buildings— only low partitions between learning areas. But the mind can build walls too, and Brookdale was determined not to erect these.

The career programs would be integrated with the transfer programs; there would be no "second-class citizens." The college's programs would be divided into four institutes: Business, Human Affairs, Science, and Humanities. Eventually, it was planned, each Institute would have its own campus building. But each Institute would contain both career and transfer programs. In Science, for example, would be grouped both Automotive Technology and transfer programs in Chemistry and Biology.

There was another important sense in which Brookdale would be a college without walls—it would welcome as students any Monmouth County citizens possessing a high school diploma or equivalency certificate. In fact, the admissions policy adopted on March 19, 1969, placed admissions on a "first come, first served" basis.

"Open admissions" conjures up in some minds a disdain for "wasting" educational resources on those who are not "college material." However, admission to Brookdale did not guarantee admission to all programs. In some programs, students lacking minimal skills were required to take remedial or "developmental" courses before tackling the regular course work. In addition, each entering student was given placement tests and guided into the programs best suited to his or her ability. Brookdale has never seen any benefit in denying the necessary training to someone who has the potential to be, for instance, a first-rate auto mechanic, simply because he cannot read the *Aeneid* in Latin.

Dr. Harlacher gives the most eloquent defense of Brookdale's admissions policy:

> Brookdale's Master Plan would tend to emulate the Hospital Model to which institutions of higher learning have often been compared because both college and hospital are characterized by diagnosis and treatment of human needs. The chief distinction between the two types has always been that hospitals have prescribed different treatment for different patients; whereas colleges have given all students the same lecture/textbook treatment. . . .
>
> The inevitable result has been that learners slow to achieve have become frustrated and discouraged, and either dropped or flunked out. . . .
>
> We do not claim, or even pretend, that every student who enters our open door is a potential Phi Beta Kappa. We do claim, and vigorously defend our position, that every student has the right to the services the college provides in helping him discover latent aptitudes and interests, and how far and how fast he can go toward becoming all that he is capable of becoming.[3]

By April, 1969, Shaver and Kellenyi had completed their plans to transform the stables into permanent campus buildings. The architects were eager to begin the actual work. But there were forty-one problems standing in their way: forty high-strung race horses and one angry horse trainer, Thomas P. Harroway.

In fact, the architects had trouble getting into the barns to take measurements. "We had the plans finished, we had a contract awarded, but the horses were still in the barn," Kellenyi explains.

> And the horses were very delicate, and the owner would not let us do anything in the barns to disturb the horses. . . . [Harroway] pointed out very particularly that some of these horses were worth a couple of hundred thousand dollars, and he didn't want them to get excited and bruise their legs or something because they were jumping around in the stall.[4]

"I don't know whether you ever had a job of where to put forty horses," Tom Auch lamented.

Here was Tom [Harroway] who had contracts with people to train their horses ... for the horse racing season. ... Yet in order to be ready by September we had to have the barns by April to let the contractors in to start remodeling. This meant simply that we had to help Tom Harroway to find a place for housing the horses. That became my responsibility. We were assisted by Jim Truncer and the County Park System. It so happened that they had a forty-horse stable over there. ... The Freeholders and Jim Truncer and John Pillsbury and I organized a kind of agreement which allowed us on April 8, the day before the contractors came in here, to move all forty horses across the field into these stables over there in the County Park. ... We had to ride some of the horses. We actually had to get on their backs and ride them across.[5]

The horses being ridden out of the barns so that renovation can begin.

"The horses left, but getting rid of the flies was another thing," Shirley Zeisel interjects.[6] And the flies came back every spring for about six years, presumably from force of habit. However, back in April, 1969, they had a definite reason for being there. A distinct aroma of horse remained in the barns.

It was then that Kellenyi's experience in remodeling barns came to the fore:

> I remember that at the time Shaver was all excited. But at Christian Brothers we had the same problem. . . . We took the first six inches of dirt out of the floor . . . and took it away. And they'd come in with deodorizers and put them in the ground, then spray the building . . . and initially we found there was a little bit of an odor in the woodwork. . . .
>
> But another part of the barns that is interesting [is] the woodwork on the side walls [and the woodwork] in the stalls . . . where the edges were chewed off by the horses . . . and there were some places where they kicked it. . . . We scraped it off and then refinished it. But the marks were kept there. . . . The one thing we got rid of was the odor.[7]

They even kept the corncrib, which Marvin Clark jovially refers to as "Clark Hall." In fact, moving the corncrib was the one real extravagance the founders of Brookdale permitted themselves. It is huge, forming two arcades for students to pass through on the way from Barn B to the Performing Arts Center. They relax there on benches, or use it as a shelter from the rain.

Brookdale's corncrib in its permanent location on the campus.

"Mac" Clark was happy to explain what a corncrib is and why he calls it "Clark Hall":

A corncrib was . . . where you stored corn. It's a slanted structure that has a roof on it, so the rain won't come in from the top, but the air can get in from the sides. . . . So the crib was moved over there, and the bill came, and I think it was three or four thousand dollars for relocating this corncrib. I blew my stack because I said that I hoped the farmers of Monmouth County never found out that I was part of moving that old corncrib for three thousand dollars when we could have built a new one for three hundred! So. . . . in deference to my opinion, they said that they would name it Clark Hall.[8]

Bernard Kellenyi said that, like so much at Brookdale, keeping the corncrib was Ervin Harlacher's idea: "The corncrib was one of Harlacher's real pets. . . . It was part of the farm. . . . It was taken as such a nice thing, such nostalgia, a real old horse farm. . . . I think it turned out to be something very nice that people see and talk about."[9]

It would be hard to lay a cornerstone in a building that is already there, and a cornerstone would not be of much use in a barn. Question: What kind of ceremony should be held to inaugurate a college with hoof marks on the walls and a $3,000 corncrib? Answer: A barn raising. (In this traditional early American ceremony, all the neighbors came to break a bottle of rum over the barn's ridgepole.)

Brookdale decided to combine the best features of a barn raising and a cornerstone-laying. Accordingly, on May 28, 1969, Freeholder Director Joseph Irwin and General W. Preston Corderman, in a public ceremony, placed plans of the college, autographed by about 100 people instrumental in planning the college, into a grain chute in one of the barns and nailed it shut. (Mr. Irwin still had his doubts, and he made a bet on the spot with Dr. Harlacher that the renovation would not work out.)

Much has been said about the way Dr. Harlacher wanted the form of the learning areas to follow their function, but no one has summed up better than Bernard Kellenyi the intimate way in which the new president's vision shaped the architects' planning:

> He had the philosophy that when students came to the community college they . . . should not necessarily know what they wanted to do with the rest of their lives or how they wanted to study. So he wanted to get them in there, but . . . to make them expose themselves to other avenues of learning. . . . He wanted us to design the building so if someone was there and he thought he ought to . . . study Business that he could be able to just walk around and look over . . . and see the art students working, with the idea that it's not as bad as we thought, and maybe we could do that. The same thing with every different kind of learning. He wanted it to be as [if] they would have to walk by a lecture . . . and half listen to the lecture. Maybe the next term they would think, "I should have been studying that." So that kind of thought went into the campus . . . and is one of the reasons that the balcony's there. . . . The first floor is all . . . laboratories . . . and up above were all the Learning Resources and group learning area. . . . Almost everybody would be assigned to something on the upper floor and . . . they would have the opportunity to walk near the balcony and see what was down there.[10]

That summer of 1969, there was not enough usable building space on the Lincroft campus to hold the burgeoning staff and faculty. The former County Vocational Institute at the old NIKE base provided a central base of operations. The equipment from the vocational programs already there was to prove a boon—though it meant that staff members had to be careful not to walk into an auto lift! As Earl Garrison pointed out, vocational-technical programs are enormously more expensive than most straight academic programs because they require specialized machinery and equipment. The equipment for the college's first year vocational programs, except for Allied Health and Nursing, was already present at the NIKE base. Area hospitals provided facilities for the para-medical fields.

Arrangements were also being made for the use of nine other locations—several high schools, the Red Bank Methodist Church, and the Sandy Hook marine laboratory—for part-time day and evening extension courses and the non-credit courses to be offered by Community Services.

The basic curriculum had been settled, but it was unresolved just how far self-paced individualized learning could be implemented the first year. The basic idea of self-paced learning is obvious. Charles L. Morgan, the college's former legal counsel, describes the concept in a few pithy sentences:

The basic concept that was new in education was based on a very simple principle: everybody . . . learns at a different rate. And when you take thirty people and put them in a class . . . they've got to master a certain amount of material in a certain amount of time. And if they get seventy percent of it they pass. The Brookdale concept was . . . we don't want to give them seventy percent of it, we want to give them 100 percent of it. It may take one guy longer than another. Now that's a simple statement . . . but to implement it . . . it's a very difficult concept.[11]

Ervin Harlacher once boiled down Brookdale's concept of mastery learning into one memorable image: "We want to eliminate the 'B minus' auto mechanic. He gets an 'A' in taking the car apart and a 'D' in putting it back together, and it averages out to a 'B minus.'"[12]

The difficulty in putting the Brookdale idea into practice stemmed from the fact that, with self-pacing, the slower learners would not be finished by the end of the term. When this happened, should they have to start over again? It was a knotty problem that the college did not solve overnight.

Open space instruction was another new concept. Although there had been considerable open-space construction in elementary and high schools, it had not been used to any great extent in colleges. This meant that most of the college-level faculty at Brookdale had neither used self-paced instruction nor taught in open space. How much could they be expected to adapt in the first year?

Brookdale's faculty was introduced to such concepts as self-pacing, mastery learning, and student-centered instruction in an orientation program that took up the early part of the summer. The program was held at the NIKE base. In August and early September, they held workshops to shape specific courses. (There would be no need to provide for a sophomore class. The contract with Monmouth College was renewed for another year so that the Brookdale students who started there could complete their sophomore year and graduate from Monmouth College.)

Brookdale had completed the first step toward academic accreditation by the Middle States Association of Colleges and Secondary Schools (MSA) without fanfare in December, 1968. On June 4, 1969, the college announced that Brookdale had scaled the second hurdle and been granted Correspondent Status by the MSA. An MSA spokesman explained that this level of recognition "attests that an institution has given evidence of sound planning and of having the resources to implement its plans." Brookdale was nothing if not planned. The Master Plan developed by GLC and Max Tadlock, a planner who had subcontracted for the educational portions of the plan, filled four thick volumes when completed and covered almost everything except how much to charge for a bag of potato chips in the vending machines.

Preparatory to the September 29 opening of classes, the college announced that its full-time faculty of fifty-four was complete and that the part-time faculty was being recruited. The part-time program, like the non-credit Community Services courses being started by Dean Clinton Crocker, reflected the determination of the president and trustees to begin with a full-scale "outreach" program to bring Brookdale's educational opportunities to everyone who wanted them.

As Audrie LaTowsky puts it, "The biggest trauma the whole time . . . was were we going to meet our building deadlines . . . so that we could admit more students. . . . We had students pounding at our doors. . . . We did take everybody. There was no cut-off. We made room. We opened extension centers. . . . We used every nook and cranny we could use."[13]

There was a flurry of behind-the-scenes activity in preparation for the college's September 29 opening. Media specialist Martha Thompson said, "There was a high *esprit de corps* at that time. Everybody wanted to see everything in order. And we had faculty members, their wives, their children, volunteers from AAUW—all these people came in and spent hours of their spare time."[14]

On the 29th, Monmouth County dignitaries and college officials opened the school with a champagne toast. Some of the students had been dubious about going to school in over-hauled stables. But when they saw the gold carpeting, the in-direct lighting, the fine wood paneling (complete with hoof marks!), and the real horse stalls in the eating area, they were openly delighted. Student Frank Gagliano of Oakhurst was entranced. "Those beams give the place a warm feeling, kind of cozy," he said. "I think the library is my favorite room. It's got an old-fashioned look, but very modern where it should be, in the facilities. Everything's close-knit, informal. . . . I was expecting dingy old shacks. Am I ever happy with this!"[15]

Joseph Irwin had lost his bet, and no one was happier about it than he, because the people of Monmouth County were the real winners. "I must hand it to them," he mused, referring to Dr. Harlacher's "miracle workers."[16]

Ervin Harlacher summed it up: "Some people call our little operation 'the impossible dream.' It was, but it wasn't im-possible . . . it was a dream that materialized."[17]

A class in one of the renovated barns in the Fall of 1969.

The average age of the full-time freshman class was under twenty-one. The percentage of older students was higher in the part-time extension program. This program was the start of college for Mrs. Lucille Lubow, a woman in her forties whose fate has been intertwined with Brookdale's since her undergraduate days. Mrs. Lubow is now a learning assistant in the mathematics department, and she is just completing her part-time studies toward a Bachelor's degree at Kean College. Although Mrs. Lubow was valedictorian of the Class of 1971 at Brookdale, she was not sure whether she could handle college. But she felt she should try.

In her job as part-time naturalist for the County Parks System, she often took school and college groups on nature tours of the parks. "I found we were getting kids out of college with Biology degrees, and I was training them," she explained. "I didn't like the looks of it. I said, 'Lucille, you had better get to college and get a Biology degree.'"[18] So she signed up for three off-campus courses. After her second term, more confident of her ability, she matriculated. Meanwhile, her son has graduated from Brookdale, and her daughter will matriculate in the fall of 1977.

Another of Brookdale's first students, Karl Fox, now a Management Specialist for Monmouth County, had never thought of himself as college material. He had moved fourteen times during his childhood, and he felt his learning ability had suffered. When he came to Brookdale he was a married Vietnam War veteran in his early twenties.

Fox enrolled in the Business program, with the idea of becoming an accountant. However, Brookdale's open atmosphere—just as Dr. Harlacher had intended—exposed him to other study and career avenues: "There were occupations I came across that I didn't know existed . . . like grants management. People actually go out and raise funds professionally. That was something I wasn't aware of earlier, but after leaving Brookdale I went into it."[19]

While completing his Bachelor's degree at Stockton State College, Fox interned at Brookdale for a term in Student Activities. After graduation from Stockton, he returned to

Brookdale to work in the president's office as a grantsman, one who searches out financial grants for the college.

Mrs. Anita Clax, married and the mother of five children, two of them in high school, knew exactly what she wanted to do with her life. She wanted to help people with "mental problems." Mrs. Clax had had a year of college in New Orleans and a year at the Howard University School of Nursing in Washington, D. C. But she had not been able to become a registered nurse and, in 1969, was working as a licensed practical nurse at Marlboro Psychiatric Hospital. Because of her academic background, her length of service, and the high quality of her work, Marlboro offered her a scholarship to Brookdale that year to fulfill her lifelong "impossible dream" of becoming a registered nurse.

Psychiatric nursing takes special qualities of tolerance, patience, and understanding. Anita had realized that she wanted to work in this field while living in Washington, D.C., many years ago: "When I was in Washington . . . , I lived with a family who had a mentally retarded child, and the mother didn't exactly know how to deal with this child. I would help her with the child, and it . . . gave me the idea that if I ever went into nursing . . . I could help someone with a mental problem."[20]

Mrs. Clax received her R. N. and Associate degrees from Brookdale in June, 1971. Today she is a Staff Nurse in the Medical-Surgical Department at Marlboro. Her next goal is to achieve the rank of Head Nurse.

Several times at Brookdale Anita became discouraged, but two of her professors—Frank Gimble, her Anatomy and Physiology instructor, and Mrs. Pat Connors, her Nursing instructor—would not let her quit. Neither would her family: "At my age . . . it was hard for me to get back in the routine of studying and having to take care of the house and children. Mr. Gimble would come and say to me, 'Now listen, Anita! I know it's hard, but you've got to stick with it.' And I would come in and get extra help from him in the afternoons. Pat Connors would take me some nights. . . . My husband would help me some nights. My eldest daughter was very, very good.

She is now a pre-med at Rutgers University, and she is a very good teacher."[21]

Both Karl Fox and Anita Clax have vivid recollections of the opening days on campus. Karl in particular remembers the flies: "It took the flies about eight months to realize it wasn't a barn any more. In September, both floors of the present Administration Building were academic: on the second floor were typing and accounting classes; down below were other classrooms and the cafeteria. The flies were just horrendous. I guess they had used the place for years, and in September they didn't know they should have left."[22]

Anita found the open-space idea distracting:

We had two buildings, Barn A and Barn B. We'd walk in the rain, and they did not have a lawn, just mud. You smelled odor from the [horses] that were on the farm, even in the classroom. The classrooms were divided by partitions. It was very disturbing to hear a professor in the next area talking to his students.[23]

The faculty and staff had their problems, too. Media specialist Elinor Ebeling, describes some of them:

All we had between open classroom spaces were flimsy walls. People were howling at each other vying for the student's attention. We in the library were on a balcony above where all this was going on in the classes. To try to have a library or Learning Resources Center where all this activity was going on was disconcerting, to say the least. All of us had a learning experience that first year. . . . If you lived through that first year or two, you learrned how to get along in open spaces. You had to . . . take the important head work home with you, because you couldn't get anything done . . . at your desk. . . . In both the barns we were very, very close and very tight and very much together. I think a lot of that togetherness feeling has gone as . . . the buildings have been built. We at least have desk areas we can call our own, sort of a quiet area.[24]

Even Ervin Harlacher is quick to admit that the first year was difficult, crowded, and noisy. He explains why:

The facilities were designed for the individualized approach to instruction, where the students would essentially learn on their own, using . . .

learning objectives ... having lectures in other facilities that were equipped for lectures, that were sound-proof. . . . But the strategies and modes of instruction that were employed in the first year were very traditional. This was done deliberately, because we felt that the faculty was not yet ready to move into the totally individualized . . . . What we essentially had the first year were faculty members lecturing in open space.[25]

Dr. Harlacher says that the second year, when some programs were moved to the NIKE base and two smaller barns were opened, there was more lecture space and the noise problem abated. People were providing individualized instruction. Lectures were held in lecture halls, and the seminar spaces were used for discussion groups.

Fox recalls that some of the students "didn't adjust too well," but he believes that learning by objectives and individualized pacing has, in general, worked out well.

It taught a lot of students to be self-starters, rather than to be led through an academic process [Fox observed]. It kicked them in the behind and said, "Now, you do it yourself." I saw this quite amusingly when about five of us transferred to Stockton. A professor said down there, "I can always tell a Brookdale student because they sit in the front of the room and not the back." I think that meant a lot—the fact that they wanted to learn, and they were going to get in there and fight to learn.[26]

When students had complaints, they were able to take them right to the top. Dr. Harlacher had frequent coffee hours and "rap sessions" with the students. In addition, from the very beginning students actually took part in the college's system of governance—on committees with actual administrative powers—right beside staff and faculty. Karl Fox was very active in this system.

There were growing pains [he says], in the sense that students, faculty, and administrators grew together. . . . Being a college of about 1,200, there were a lot of committees. And, oh, if I look back, I think I probably served on twenty different committees, ranging from searching for vice-presidents to facilities to everything else.[27]

Twice in the first year, successful interaction between students and the administration was demonstrated dramatically.

The first crisis, in February, 1970, was caused by a berserk computer. The computer created chaos with the registration. The college had held classes from 7:30 a.m. to 10:30 p.m. the first term, and now it was trying to condense the class schedule to fit the hours between 8:30 a.m. and 5:30 p.m. There were also about 100 more students—Lucille Lubow among them—matriculating for the second term.

The computer apparently found these changes beyond its ken. About 200 students received no schedules at all, after two weeks of daily waiting in the Administration Building Other students signed up for five courses and were scheduled for three. Tom Auch has good reason to remember the computer crisis, because he was right in the middle of it:

There were eighty students in one class and three in another class. They were told to go someplace at a certain time, and there was no class meeting there. . . . The students were very unhappy about this. . . . At that time too there was a great deal . . . of campus unrest, student demonstrations. Also, we were bothered by Cambodia and Kent State. These things all came to a head at one time. . . . They kind of started storming the Administration Building. At this one particular time Erv had gone out of town. . . . He had left me in charge. We were sitting around talking one day because the students were making threats about coming to converge on the president and hanging him in effigy. We were sitting in this very office, and I was saying to myself, "The poor president." And I suddenly realized he had gone and I was the acting president.[28]

Karl remembers the incident well as an example of the students' participating in the administrative process:

I think they burned the computer in effigy, because it was just a mess. I can remember Fred Hazlett standing down with Tom Auch in front of about 500 totally mad students waving their registration forms. They didn't know where to go, what to do about the computer. Fred was so mad, he was waving about a stack of "Add-Drop" forms that he was mad about: "If everybody would stop adding and dropping, maybe we could find out what courses to go to." We got that straightened out because three students went up and said, "Look, the registration is a mess, and we've got a better way of doing it." And he listened. . . . We got about thirty students to work the whole registration, to man the lines—marshalls. And we had them helping to fill out registration forms, and registration the next semester went very well.[29]

Today, those who remember "the registration crisis" look back on it and laugh. The Vietnam War, however, was no laughing matter. Neither was the way student protests tore this country's campuses apart, bringing the educational process to a halt and bringing death to four students at Kent State University.

It did not happen that way at Brookdale. In fact, this particular crisis—after a few tense, uncertain days—became a demonstration of unity in diversity, of tolerance and mutual respect, that should have made headlines from coast to coast. It did not, but it should have.

Tension was in the air the morning of May 6, 1970. Just after midnight the stud barn slated for remodeling into a "little theater" had burned to the ground. An anti-war debate and demonstration was scheduled for that same day. There was a question in the minds of everyone, especially the Middletown police: Had the fire been set? In retrospect it seems clear that the fire was a ghastly coincidence. A severe electrical storm had passed over the campus at the time the barn caught fire, and the blaze had started in the roof—just where lightning would be most likely to strike.

The anti-war debate went on as planned, in an emotionally-charged atmosphere. At the end of the day, 200 students at the rather sparsely attended rally voted to boycott classes in protest against the bombing of Cambodia and the Kent State killings. When the student leaders of the Strike Now Committee, Michael Fugee, Jr., Sam Staten, and Steve Swieter, met with Dr. Harlacher after the boycott vote, one of their first proposals was a fund to rebuild the barn and dedicate it to the slain Kent State students. The committee pledged its opposition to violence, confrontation, and destruction.

The president dealt with the situation in a manner consist-

A rally being held on the campus in May of 1970 between the present Admissions and Administration building and the Performing Arts Center.

ent with Brookdale's respect for the individual. "Brookdale will be nonconformist and not shut down," he asserted. Classes were to remain in session, giving students a free choice between attending them and boycotting them. He also refrained from taking a public stand on either the war or the Cambodian bombing. "As a college president," he stated, "it is my responsibility to represent all points of view on the campus of a county with all points of view."[30]

Only 300 students had attended the rally, and the opposing viewpoint immediately made itself heard. Karl Fox was one of thirty-seven students, most of them veterans, who, less than an hour after the strike was voted, formed a group called Concerned Citizens for a Moderate Brookdale. Under the chairmanship of John Pierson, Concerned Citizens attracted many students of varying political persuasions who were, whatever their view of the war, united in their aim to keep the school open.

Strike Now found little support for its boycott and reacted in the true Brookdale spirit. Mr. Fugee said:

[Strike Now] actually changed position once we got major feedback from the students, faculty, and administration. We thought participating in a national student strike would be a visible means of bringing political pressure on President Nixon. Then we found that we weren't being supported and that we infringed on the rights of others. . . . We decided immediately to end the polarity and to find other means to demonstrate our protest. The Concerned Students came to us through the Student Government, and we're glad they did.[31]

Tolerance like this was undoubtedly unique to Brookdale that spring. By May 13, Strike Now had changed its name and reorganized as the Work for Peace Committee. Concerned Students disbanded. John Pierson said that he expected some of its members would join Work for Peace. Steve Swieter and John Pierson, with a beaming Ervin Harlacher between them, shook hands under a huge banner proclaiming, "We're Together."

In another remarkable show of unity, Pierson and Swieter announced that they would manage jointly the campaign of a slate of officers for the student government elections in June: Karl Fox of Concerned Students for president, and Michael Fugee of Work for Peace for vice-president.

When the students journeyed to Newark with photographs and a news release, they failed to arouse the interest of the Associated Press. John Pierson bitterly recounted the wire service's reaction: "They told us it was a regional story and too peaceful, but that if we have a riot the A. P. would come down and cover it."[32]

At first it appeared that the loss of the stud barn would seriously set back the college's building program. The "little theater," seating 200, was to have doubled as much-needed lecture space.

Fortunately the barn had been insured. With their usual flair, Dr. Harlacher and the board of trustees decided once more to attempt the impossible. Bernard Kellenyi recalled,

We had a crash program where we designed the new theater almost overnight. And the college received their insurance money, and they built the barn and had it open in time for the students in September. Yes, Brookdale made us 'burn a little midnight oil' at times. Any time they wanted to do something, they didn't want to wait.[33]

Indeed, the administration let very little grass grow under its feet that first year. Ervin Harlacher wanted the whole county as the campus; and with extension centers spreading through the county like branches from a tree, the county really *was* the campus. Making the whole population the student body would take a little longer.

Many county residents lacked the high school diploma or equivalency certificate needed for matriculation, but they were not to be ignored by Brookdale. On November 3, 1969, the college approved a $3,000 a year lease to take over the vacant Liberty Street School in Long Branch. This was the beginning of the Long Branch Learning Center. Brookdale qualified for a state grant to open and run it under the Neighborhood Education Center Act of 1968. The center would provide tutorial services for full-time Brookdale students from the community, counseling for community residents, and programs to meet other community needs.

Under the direction of Dean Clinton Crocker, Brookdale's Community Services division was offering nearly thirty non-credit courses. Some examples: scuba diving for policemen; a course on public subsidies, for low-income families; "Marriage: Merger or Mayhem," for married couples of all ages; and "Ethics: Dilemma for Modern Man."

The part-time credit program, by January, 1970, was offering 118 sections of sixty-seven different courses. A few of these were administered by Community Services, and even today certain credit programs are run by Community Services.

An important point about the non-credit Community Services offerings, which was true then and is still true now when Community Services offers about eighty-five or ninety courses each term, is that the courses are financially self-supporting. Robert W. Leonard, the present Dean of Community Services, explains the principle:

What the college does pay for is my staff. It does not pay for any of the courses that we run. It doesn't pay for any of the faculty. . . . [The fees charged for the courses] pay for everything we do. . . . And then all the money that we make, we just put back into Community Services again by using [it] to develop new courses, new programs. ... We pay for our own printing, our own mailing, our own supplies.[34]

Brookdale's contribution to Monmouth County's cultural life began in that first year also. Monmouth Museum, which had been operating in temporary quarters, had been considering the Brookdale campus as the site for a permanent facility since the summer of 1969. On March 23, 1970, the college's board of trustees approved an agreement allowing the museum a thirty-year lease on a one-acre site on campus for an annual rental of one dollar. The tract was located near a twenty-five-acre nature area west of the main campus. On this acreage the museum undertook development of nature trails in cooperation with Brookdale's nature club. The trails were open to the public by May.

In April, Brookdale mounted its first drama workshop, presenting two original plays by Brookdale faculty members William Watkins and Eduardo Garcia. In May, the college's first full-scale dramatic production, Jean Giraudeaux' fantasy, "The Enchanted," was presented at the Old Mill Inn.

Plans were under way for expansion of the curriculum in

A view across the campus from the corncrib, showing the academic complex with the Instructional Materials Center on the left.

the fall. Courses at the sophomore level were, of course, to be added in all subject areas. On the basis of community needs, a new two-year degree program in Law Enforcement was approved by the trustees. This was designed to improve the professional opportunities of police officers. The one-year diploma program in Automotive Technology was upgraded to a two-year program leading to the degree of Associate in Applied Sciences. Two courses in Hotel-Motel Management—needed in a resort area like Monmouth County—were also added.

Brookdale even began an intercollegiate sports program in the spring of 1970, in tennis, golf, and baseball. The baseball team, the "Jersey Blues," has over the years gained recognition as a first-rate college baseball team. John Montefusco, the National League's Rookie of the Year in 1975, broke in his dazzling pitches with the "Blues." In 1976, another Brookdale hurler, Doug Smith, signed with the Boston Red Sox. It is not unheard of for talented baseball players to turn down athletic scholarships at other colleges to play with Brookdale's powerhouse team. Today, Brookdale offers many opportunities for collegiate athletes, including soccer, basketball, rugby, wrestling, and women's tennis.

In May, 1970, the Middle States Association named Brookdale a Recognized Candidate for Accreditation. This third step in the accreditation process was tantamount to full accreditation within the state of New Jersey. Rutgers University had already announced, in February, that it would consider Brookdale graduates for acceptance as transfer students.

In June of the same year, Brookdale held its first graduation ceremony, for a handful of vocational students who had begun their education under the County Vocational Institute. In July, forty-two women who had started their nursing education at the Monmouth Medical Center School of Nursing also became Brookdale graduates.

The degree program in Automotive Technology that Brookdale was developing was to go far toward eliminating Ervin Harlacher's "B minus auto mechanic." Karl Fox

The campus street from the Natural and Applied Sciences Institute, looking toward the College Commons at the right.

once heard a local auto dealer say, "I spend $60,000 a year training my people. And if I can get a graduate from Brookdale who has two years [he] not only knows what is wrong with the car but knows the theory behind it. Plus he is able to speak well to my customers and write well."[35]

Dr. Harlacher dubbed 1969-70 "the year of the student." It was a good year, one of many impressive beginnings, one in which cooperation had prevailed over partisan ardor. In a July editorial, the *Daily Register* summed up the feelings of a great many Monmouth County residents:

Monmouth County has, in Brookdale Community College, an outstanding example of the contribution a community college can make in its area. In a single year of operation it has become an indispensable element of our sociocultural community. Already we wonder how we did without it.[16]

Work on one stud barn and a new building to replace the other proceeded over the summer, and the college began to look forward to the realization of Phase II of its architectural Master Plan. Entirely new buildings would house the Institute of Applied Humanities and the Institute of Human Affairs. Science programs had adequate facilities at the NIKE base. A new lecture hall and an instructional materials center were also planned. When those buildings were completed, half of the proposed physical plant would be finished. The target date was September, 1971.

The next September, Karl Fox took office as student body president. By this time, Lucille Lubow, who had always "dreaded math," was a mathematics major. She attributes her switch from biology to math to the high quality of mathematics instruction at Brookdale and her love of a challenge: "I became terribly interested in math, and I liked it here. How could you not like it here? So I decided to change my major to math. It comes harder to me than biology. I get more pleasure out of achieving something that is difficult."[37]

During the second year additional progress was made toward individualized instruction. Lucille remembers that the faculty and the Instructional Materials Center spent much of their time the first year making up the "learning packages" required for the new teaching technique. These "packages" used slides, film, taped narration, and other nonprint media to teach course material. It was then possible for a student to use the "learning package" on his own in the Learning Resources Center.

Laboratories for the assistance of students were also being established in many Learning Centers such as Mathematics and Writing. Lucille Lubow explains her job as Learning Assistant:

The Math Lab is a place where any student taking a math course may come to get help. . . . We grade tests. We hand out learning packages. If we notice that students are having special problems, we will refer them to their teacher. . . . A student might have a homework assignment, and he is having a little difficulty with it, and we help him with it. . . . It is not our job to be a private tutor, to sit with someone for five hours, because we have hundreds of students.[38]

A year after its opening, the Long Branch Learning Center was a resounding success. Under the direction of Edward Davis, it was "turning on" disillusioned, discouraged, inner-city residents of all ages to education. 117 people of all ethnic backgrounds were enrolled in four free educational programs. The first program was for those, young and old, who wished to earn a high school diploma. Later the Center would become a Federal and state agency for high school equivalency testing in English and Spanish.

A second program, for the benefit of the Spanish-speaking community, was English as a Second Language.

The third offering was a power sewing course, using machines donated by the ILGWU, to train people to use industrial sewing machines. This skill would enable them to take jobs in the Long Branch area's needle trades.

The fourth program was a college preparatory sequence for high school graduates. Those who completed these basic courses would be prepared to matriculate at Brookdale.

In addition to these special programs, Brookdale was offering six courses for college credit at the Learning Center.

The Community Services program continued to grow and was serving hundreds of people each term—including the summer months—with courses ranging from the chilling of wine to sign language for parents of deaf children. Community Services was there to cater to people's lightest moments and to serve their deepest needs. The fact that the courses were self-supporting led to a flexible and imaginative roster of offerings.

The success of a college can best be measured by the achievements of its students. On June 27, when the Class of 1971 graduated at the Garden State Arts Center, Lucille Lubow, the woman who had not been sure she could handle college, graduated first in a class of 306. At the graduation, Karl Fox, newly-elected President of the Brookdale Alumni Association, presented the class gift. Anita Clax was one of fifty-seven nurses who graduated that day, with R. N. and A. A. S. degrees.

Brookdale was well pleased with the work of Ervin Harlacher and renewed his contract for another three years. He was well pleased with his "impossible dream," and had reason to be. In 1970-71, thirty-eight percent of the students' grades were credit with high honors or honors, and twenty-two percent were at the credit level. The attrition rate was a mere thirteen percent—phenomenally low for a community college. If anything marred the rosy picture, it was the large number of incompletes—totalling twenty-five percent—which were not included in the statistics because they represented grades given to slow learners. This problem was the reason for the introduction of deferred credit.

Another of Dr. Harlacher's disappointments would have been shocking coming from the president of a traditional junior college. He had hoped that more students would enroll in the occupational programs. Only about thirty percent of the class intended to go directly into jobs. "It should be the other way around," he lamented. "Seventy percent should be going into occupational programs."[39] Today the balance has shifted to the point that half of Brookdale's students pursue career training programs.

Trustee Dr. Joseph E. Clayton sees the positive results of Brookdale's occupational programs wherever he goes in Monmouth County:

I talk with them. The boy who puts gas in my car goes to Brookdale. I find out a lot from him. . . . The girl that works in the dentist's office graduated from Brookdale. . . . My daughter was in the hospital with pneumonia . . . and the girl that was doing the therapy was taking her training at Brookdale. . . . She couldn't say enough about the program that she had over there. Her father was a physical therapist, and he was very proud of the program that we had over there.[40]

The Performing Arts Center, left, and the Creative Arts Center, right, and the Institute of Applied Humanities at the beginning of the campus street.

A sweeping view of part of the completed academic complex.

Brookdale had never believed that learning takes place best between the hours of nine a.m. and three p.m. in the months between September and June. While work on the new campus facilities proceeded that summer, Brookdale offered sixty summer term courses in twenty-eight subjects, most of them scheduled in the morning and evening so that students could enjoy sun and surf in the afternoon.

The second phase of the physical plant proceeded on schedule. Shaver and Kellenyi had set the basic farm theme for the campus with their brilliant remodeling of the barns. Their next artistic challenge was to design new buildings to carry the theme through, using modern materials that would harmonize with the century-old barns.

Working together, the architects arrived at the perfect "look" for the academic complex and the perfect materials in which to execute it. Kellenyi explains that they duplicated the effect of the barns' dark roof shingles with a fireproof tile that looked just like shingles. (The same tiles were, in fact, used in Williamsburg.) The architects used brick, stone, and wood in pleasing proportions, avoiding large expanses of any one material. The wood was a rough cedar, colored with a weathering stain that would fade quickly and give an "older" look.

The stones Kellenyi found were rich in New Jersey associations. They are called "Delaware Jacks," because they are stones from the bottom of the Delaware River that have been rounded off by the current.[41]

Brookdale had made a habit of meeting deadlines, and the three handsome new buildings were ready for use that fall of 1971. They were the Institute of Applied Humanities, the Institute of Human Affairs, and the Forum. They were separate structures on the ground floor but were joined on the second floor by the Learning Resources Center, which ran the length of the three buildings. The Institute of Natural and Applied Sciences was now housed in Barn A.

Selected members of the press had already viewed the buildings and were giving them rave notices. "The new buildings excite the mind and delight the eye," exclaimed the *Register*'s Doris Kulman. "The architects . . . have kept faith with the college's setting, the gently rolling hills of Brookdale Farm. . . . The Brookdale ambiance . . . has been captured here with stone, brick, and hand-hewn cedar, their ruggedness lightened by tinted glass walls and lots of open space."[42]

Brookdale was also receiving star billing nationally. The architects received a citation for excellence from the College and University Conference and Exposition, a citation for barrier-free design from the New Jersey Easter Seals Society, and a special citation for institutional interior design from Burlington House Board of Governors. A photograph of the interior of Barn A was given a two-page spread in the October 22, 1971, issue of *Life*, in an article on "New Schools at a Bargain Rate." By 1973, articles on the college's architecture had appeared in a number of periodicals including the *Journal of the AIA* (American Institute of Architects); *College Management*; *Building, Design, and Construction*; *College and University Business*; and *Tone* (a publication on acoustics).

The buildings were to be dedicated on Founders' Day.

"We had a Founders' Day in early October," Tom Auch recalls.

That meant we were going on view to the public. That was real interesting because everybody pitched in. We all came out the day before Founders' Day. And everybody had their dust rag, and their vacuum cleaners, and their paint brushes. Everybody was pitching in—the whole faculty, all the staff. . . . We had students here, and just everybody was pitching in. It was just a lot of fun.[43]

Edith Reilly will never forget that time:

On Founders' Day when we dedicated the academic complex, it was a beautiful fall day. And this was something we said about Dr. Harlacher, whenever he was having some big event like this, it dared not rain. And it didn't rain that day. . . . The setting was . . . the campus street. . . . . I remember we were collecting things to put in a box. . . . I believe there is a plaque over it now, for a cornerstone.[44]

Mrs. Katherine Neuberger was the speaker. The band played—what else?—"The Impossible Dream."

What would Geraldine Thompson's reaction have been if she had been present that day? Mary Lou Wagner, who

Dr. Donald H. Smith, President of Brookdale Community College, congratulates a member of the class of '77 at commencement exercises.

teaches sociology at Brookdale and knew Mrs. Thompson in her later years, has no doubt how that grand old lady would have felt:

I can't think of any greater tribute to a great woman such as Mrs. Thompson than to have this college on her land. She would be ecstatic. I can see her walking around here. She would totter up to students and say — in her way — "Now, how is everything? Are you learning anything?" She would say, "Well, I don't like this," and she would call the president and say that this should be done in a different way. She was always concerned about other people, always ready and willing . . . to see if she could do anything to help you.[45]

Brookdale will carry on in her spirit.

APPENDICES

APPENDIX I: Monmouth Patent Holders Who Settled in Middletown

Captain John Bowne, an ancestor of President Abraham Lincoln, had been forced out of Massachusetts, where Baptists were not welcome. He settled for a time in Gravesend, Long Island, before moving in 1663 to Monmouth County.[1] According to historian Franklin Ellis, Bowne "seems to have been the most prominent citizen of the county, esteemed for his integrity and ability."[2] He lived in Middletown (where he became a founder of the Baptist Church) until his death in 1684, and was buried in the Old Presbyterian Burying Ground. His grave marker is the oldest stone in the cemetery.[3]

John Tilton settled first in Massachusetts, where his Baptist wife was indicted for not baptizing infants. The Tiltons made their way to Long Island and then to Monmouth County, where they settled in 1665. *Richard Gibbons* and *Samuel Spicer* also came to the county from Long Island in search of religious freedom.

James Grover settled in the county in 1663, two years before the patent was granted. As the first town clerk and surveyor he was able to identify and secure for himself land rich in iron ore at "the falls in Shrewsbury." Grover hired English millwrights to build an iron works on this site.

William Reape, a Quaker, had been imprisoned on Long Island for not practicing the religion of the Dutch. He later settled in Rhode Island. When he found that Rhode Island Quakers were forced to bear arms despite their conscientious objections, Reape fled to Monmouth County.

William Goulding, like John Bowne, had been persecuted and banished from the Massachusetts Bay Colony because he was a Baptist. He settled permanently in Monmouth County and was a founder of the Middletown Baptist Church.

Richard Stout was "one of the most respectable and respected men in his day in the Monmouth settlements."[4] Legend surrounds the name of Stout's wife, Penelope, who arrived in America on a ship from Amsterdam. The ship

[1] Ernest W. Mandeville, *The Story of Middletown, the Oldest Settlement in New Jersey* (Middletown: Christ Church, 1972), p. 39.

[2] Franklin Ellis, *History of Monmouth County* (Philadelphia: R. T. Peck and Co., 1885), p. 66.

[3] Mandeville, p. 39.

[4] Ellis, p. 68.

went aground on Sandy Hook, and the passengers were stranded. Among them was a young Dutchman who had been sick for most of the voyage and was unable to make his way to New Amsterdam with the other passengers. His wife, then *Penelope Van Princes,* chose to stay with him.

As the legend has it, Penelope and her husband were attacked by Indians who killed the young man and left Penelope for dead. She nevertheless managed to survive, and was found by an elderly Indian who carried her to his village, near Middletown. After regaining her health, Penelope went to New Amsterdam where she met and married Richard Stout. When Stout established a permanent home in Middletown, Penelope was returned to the site of her narrow escape.

Penelope and Richard had seven sons and three daughters, beginning a long line of descendants who resided in the county. Today, on Crawford's Corner Road in Holmdel, there stands a house in which Penelope Stout is believed to have lived.

APPENDIX II: Some Early Owners of the Brookdale Triangle

Michael Taylor was born in Recklesstown, New Jersey, in 1820. First a blacksmith and later a farmer, Taylor acquired his Middletown property in 1869. After he sold his property to David Withers, he and his wife, Sarah Bennett Taylor, moved to the John H. Holmes farm.

Taylor was an influential member of the county Democratic Party and was a representative in the state legislature from 1862 to 1865. He also served as Freeholder and held other offices in the township. He was a founder and president of the Monmouth Agricultural Society, and in 1884 became the first president of the First National Bank of Keyport (now part of the Colonial First National Bank). While a legislator, he secured the charter for the Pemberton and Hightstown Railroad. He was a member of the Reformed (Dutch) Church of Holmdel, and was highly esteemed as a man of "business capacity and acknowledged integrity."[1]

Rulief Smock was born in 1829 of an old Monmouth County family, which had first settled in the area in 1712. His great-great uncle, Barnes Smock, was a captain of a battalion in the Monmouth County militia in 1777 and was captain of the first regiment of the Continental Army from 1776-1780.

---

[1] Franklin Ellis, *History of Monmouth County* (Philadelphia: R. T. Peck and Co., 1885), p. 47.

The Leonards, like Michael Taylor, were prominent in county farming and banking. The property sold by Sarah Leonard et al. to David Withers had been conveyed to the Leonards by Daniel and Eleanor Roberts in 1885.[2] Previous owners of this parcel were Thomas and Martha Field (conveyed in 1868),[3] the Lloyd family (conveyed in 1867),[4] Thomas and Sarah Shepard (conveyed in 1774),[5] Thomas Leeds (conveyed in 1719), and John Reid (conveyed in 1699).

Richard Leonard, born in 1812, was one of the founders of the Monmouth Agricultural Society, one of the incorporators of the First National Bank of Red Bank (now Colonial First National Bank), one of the projectors of the New Jersey Southern Railroad, and one of the founders of the Peddie Institute in Hightstown. On his death in 1877, Richard Leonard was paid tribute by the New Jersey State Temperance Alliance as "a life-long and uncompromising enemy of the iniquitous liquor traffic."[6]

Christ Church, Middletown received four hundred acres bequeathed by *William Leeds, Jr.,* who died in 1739. In 1693, William Leeds, Sr. had previously conveyed his land in Middletown to his brother, Daniel, as trustee. William, Jr., received the land from the trustee in 1715.[7]

William Leeds, Sr. and *Daniel Applegate* signed a lease dated July 16, 1684, with Iraseeke of Wickaton, Sachem (chief), the Indian owner of the land. The land was a "tract lying in Middletown or Chawcosette called Amoskake marked by my uncle Seahoppa. . . ."[8] The term of the lease was for 315 years and the annual rental was four yards of Duffield tobacco or its equivalent in rum. In 1680 William Leeds purchased the Indian rights of Cherewas-Melileth, Charles, Puropa, Lendreck, Iraseef, Mestoa, Porwas, Leoples, Secoes and Metopeek of the Scheyichbi Indians covering "a tract of land called Pessick Amesslafe which lay north and west and east of Ben Burden's Brook and Hop River and Swimming Brook. . . ."[9] In 1679 Leeds had purchased a "manour of lands" from Richard and Frances Stout.[10]

[2] Hall of Records, Deed Book 398, p. 202.

[3] Hall of Records, Deed Book 213, p. 71.

[4] Hall of Records, Deed Book 202, p. 337.

[5] Christ Church, Shrewsbury, New Jersey, Deed of Sale, July 8, 1774.

[6] Ellis, p. 558.

[7] Hall of Records, Deed Book E, p. 203.

[8] Hall of Records, Deed Book B, p. 17.

[9] Hall of Records, Deed Book C, pp. 178-79.

[10] Christ Church, Shrewsbury, Deed dated February 4, 1679.

Richard Stout was one of the original land owners under the Monmouth Patent.

APPENDIX III: *The North American Phalanx*

The North American Phalanx, a co-operative community organized in 1843, was associated with some of the leading intellectuals of the day. The idea behind the community was based on the social theory of Francois Marie Charles Fourier (1772-1837), a French social economist. He advocated that industry should be carried on by a system of phalanxes, small co-operative units, divided into series and groups, and that each group should be responsible for a certain type of work.

Albert Brisbane introduced Fourierism into the United States. Brisbane and Allen Warden organized and chose the site for the North American Phalanx. On January 1, 1844, 673 acres on the old Van Mater slave farm in the northeast part of Atlantic Township were purchased from Hendrick Longstreet and Daniel Holmes for $14,000.[1] This land, located between Hop and Yellow Brooks on the road leading to Leedsville, was "bountifully watered by springs and brooks, together with extensive marl beds."[2]

Some of the notables said to have been associated with the Phalanx are Ralph Waldo Emerson; Charles A. Dana, editor of the New York *Sun* and Assistant Secretary of War; Nathaniel Hawthorne; Horace Greeley; Lucy Stone; W. H. Channing; William Hinds; Fredrika Brener, Swedish feminist and author; James H. Martin; George B. Arnold; Dr. E. Guillandeau, teacher; Alexander Woolcott, New York drama critic; J. Warren; John Angell; and Charles Chapin. Of these people, Horace Greeley and Alexander Woolcott (who was born on the Phalanx) were probably the only ones actually to live on the Phalanx.

The members of the North American Phalanx were primarily of the middle class. Many had been businessmen who had suffered in the depression of 1837. The members, over two hundred people, all lived together in one large building, shaped like a phalanx, an ancient Greek military formation. Labors were divided into agricultural, manufacturing, and domestic categories. Division heads planned the work each night for the following day. The highest wages were paid for the least desirable work, ten to fifteen cents an hour

[1] Hall of Records, Deed Book 405, pp. 133-35.
[2] Historical Committee of Colts Neck, *History of Colts Neck,* n. d., p. 25.

being considered fair compensation. All articles were purchase
and sold to members at cost. Profits were shared and a thir
week was maintained. Living expenses, including laundry,
about two dollars per week. The North American Phalanx becai
perous, with the mill alone making as much as $24,000 annual p

Religious freedom existed in a non-sectarian atmosphere. No
tional religious services and Sunday school were conducted every

Although the purpose of the Phalanx was to dignify labor rat.
further intellectual pursuits, each member had educational oppc
the Phalanx provided a day nursery, a day school, and a night schoc
was no age or sex discrimination. Planned recreation was provided.

The utopian goals of this society were to some extent undermin
human conflicts. There is some evidence to indicate that there were disp
over the supervision of children and on the subject of religion.

In 1854, a fire destroyed the flour mill, the saw mill, the blacksmith sho
the tin shop, and much of the equipment. The insurance company which hac
insured the property went out of business at the same time. This disaster,
in addition to the existing internal difficulties, was too great to overcome,
and the Phalanx was disbanded in 1855.

APPENDIX IV: The William Payne Thompson Family

William Payne Thompson was born in Wheeling, Virginia,[1] in 1837.[2] His
parents, Judge George W. and Mrs. Elizabeth Steenrod Thompson had a
second son, Lewis, who died in the Civil War.[3] William attended Jefferson
College briefly and, in 1857, began a law practice in Fairmount,[4] West Virginia. Although he opposed secession, he served in the Confederate Army as
Colonel of the Ninth Virginia Calvary, Fairmount Group,[5] taking part in
many battles, including Bull Run. He was at Appomattox at the time of the
surrender.[6]

[1] West Virginia was awarded statehood on June 20, 1863. Prior to that date, the West Virginia territory,
which included Wheeling, was considered a segment of Virginia.

[2] "Obituary Record: Colonel William P. Thompson," New York *Times,* 4 February 1896.

[3] Elisabeth Thompson Babcock, interview at Woodbury, Long Island, New York, August 25, 1976. In
a handmade book written by Judge George W. Thompson, Lieutenant Lewis Thompson's death is said
to have resulted from leading his men up a hill defended by the Union Army, 1861.

[4] Current spelling is "Fairmont."

[5] "Obituary Record."

[6] ". . . Resident of Red Bank," New York *Herald Tribune,* 26 March 1936.

onel William Thompson married *Mary Evelyn Moffet,* member of a
guished Virginia family.[7] The couple had three children: Lewis Steen-
Thompson, born in 1865; Elizabeth Steenrod Thompson, born in 1868;
William Payne Thompson, born in 1870.

Colonel Thompson was a man of many talents. Following the Civil War,
edited a West Virginia newspaper for a short time, after which his law
actice took him to Chicago.[8] Returning to Parkersburg, West Virginia, he
came involved in the oil industry. When his firm was absorbed by John D.
Rockefeller's Standard Oil Company in 1876, Colonel Thompson was appointed a vice-president.[9] He was transferred from Cleveland, Ohio, to New
York City in 1887 and became the general manager of the National Lead
Company (Trust) in 1889.[10] His other financial and commercial undertak-
ings included directorships of the United States National Bank, the Southern
National Bank, and the Ohio River Railroad.

In January of 1896, Colonel William Thompson developed pneumonia
while on a railroad inspection trip in West Virginia. He returned to New
York, where he died on February 3, at the age of 59.[11]

Lewis Steenrod Thompson, oldest son of William and Mary Evelyn Thompson, was born October 4, 1865. After attending boarding schools in Virginia,
he graduated with honor from Virginia Military Institute and, in 1888, from
the Massachusetts Institute of Technology.[12] For two years following his
graduation he traveled around the world.

When he was twenty-one, Lewis, along with eight companions, contracted
typhoid fever. Although his friends died from the disease, Lewis, who had
also been fighting tuberculosis, survived. "The typhoid bugs, instead of kill-
ing this young man, knocked the TB bugs senseless."[13] After three years of
recuperation he began work as a civil engineer. Unfortunately, after two
months of indoor employment, he had another attack of tuberculosis, and
doctors advised "the outdoor life" as the necessary means to his survival.

---

[7] ". . . Resident of Red Bank."

[8] "Obituary Record."

[9] Red Bank *Register,* 5 February 1896.

[10] "Obituary Record."

[11] Ibid.

[12] "Mrs. Lewis S. Thompson Tells of Her Busy Life and Multiple Activities," Long Branch *Daily Record,* 18 August 1940.

[13] Babcock, letter to Philip C. Carling, June 30-July 29, 1976.

APPENDIX V: The Morgans, Livingstons and Hoyts

Geraldine Livingston Morgan was born on March 2, 1872, ii
old Astor houses on 33rd Street, New York.[1] Soon afterward
moved to Washington Square, on the north side of the park,
members of the family had homes.

From her father's side of the family, Geraldine was a descend
erations of adventurous sea captains. Elisha E. Morgan, Geraldine
grandfather, was a captain for the Ball Line, which sailed pac
between Liverpool and New York City.[2] Captain Morgan's reside
located in Old Saybrook, Connecticut. The *Welfare Reporter* note
Geraldine possessed Spanish coins which originally had been given t
grandfather on one of his voyages by Joseph Bonaparte.[3]

Geraldine's father, *William Dare Morgan,* son of Elisha Morgan, served
captain and stroke of the Yale University Crew in 1869,[4] and was valedi
torian of his college graduating class.

Geraldine Morgan's maternal forebears were the Livingstons and Hoyts,
several of whom had played active social and political roles in the New York
area. One ancestor, William Livingston, had been governor of the colony
which formerly included New York and New Jersey.[5] Other ancestors were
General Morgan Lewis and Chancellor Robert R. Livingston of Revolutionary fame.[6]

Geraldine Livingston, Geraldine L. Morgan's maternal grandmother, was
the youngest of twelve children. After her marriage to Lydig Hoyt, she
served as a member of the State Charities Aid, showed interest in prison reform, and worked for the City of New York as a member of the Board for
Randalls Island Institution.[7] She and Miss Louisa Schuyler played a vital
part in removing the insane from the New York poorhouses and establishing

---

[1]"Mrs. Lewis S. Thompson Tells of Her Busy Life and Multiple Activities," Long Branch *Daily Record,*
18 August 1940.

[2]Elisabeth Thompson Babcock, note to Linda Lott Rizzo, July 2, 1977.

[3]"Profile: Mrs. Thompson of Brookdale Farm," *Welfare Reporter* (New Jersey Department of Institutions and Agencies, June 1950), p. 6.

[4]Ibid.

[5]"Women's Statements Bring to Close Monmouth Drive," n. p., n. n., 5 February 1931.

[6]Babcock, interview at Woodbury, Long Island, New York, August 25, 1976.

[7]"Women's Statements. . . ."

n special mental hospitals.[8] In addition, Mrs. Hoyt became the found-
president of the Social Service Department of Bellevue Hospital.[9]

liam Dare Morgan and *Angelica Livingston Hoyt Morgan* (daughter of
g and Geraldine Livingston Hoyt) had four children: Margaret, Ruth,
ldine, and Gerald. "The Morgans had little money, but what they lacked
inancial resources, they made up in dynamic energy."[10] Angelica Morgan
lowed in the footsteps of her mother, Geraldine Hoyt, in public service.
ith her aunt, Mrs. Alexander Hamilton, she organized the first training
hool for nurses at Bellevue Hospital in New York.[11]

When the Morgan children were young, they spent winters in New York
City, where Geraldine and her sisters, Margaret and Ruth, were schooled by
private tutors. Geraldine's father died when she was fourteen years old. In
the year following Mr. Morgan's death, the three girls attended the Sacre
Coeur convent school in Tours, France.

Attempting to find relief from her tuberculosis, Geraldine Livingston Morgan spent the winter of 1896 in Colorado Springs, where she met her future
husband, Lewis Thompson.

APPENDIX VI: Horses at Brookdale

For a brief period in the early 1900's, Brookdale's stable facilities were
leased to James R. Keene, a racing rival of William C. Whitney. James G.
Rowe, Sr., was the trainer. Mr. Keene's champions included Commando,
Delhi, Sysonby, Court Dress, Peter Pan, Ballot, Colin, Celt, Maskette, and
Sweep.[1]

When Mr. Keene vacated the premises, Harry Payne Whitney leased the
Brookdale tracks and stables. *The Thoroughbred Record* of November 20,
1915, recorded Brookdale's equine population as "... twenty-nine weanlings,
thirty-eight yearlings, sixty-seven broodmares, and thirty-six race horses in
training."[2]

[8]"Mrs. Lewis S. Thompson Tells . . . ."

[9]Babcock interview.

[10]William Barclay Harding, "Geraldine Thompson — Lifetime of Dedication and Service," *Daily Register,*
26 January 1965.

[11]"Women's Statements . . . ."

[1]*The Blood-Horse* (17 January 1970), p. 267.

[2]*The Thoroughbred Record* (20 November 1915), p. 248.

Wilfred Mullin, Brookdale Farm's accountant and later Greentree Stables' assistant horse trainer, recalls that among the famous stallions at Brookdale were Hamburg, Organ Minister, Pennant, and Chico.[3] Elisabeth Thompson Babcock remembers Irish Lad, Whiskbroom (II), Regret, Bostonian, Top Flight, Whichone, Equipoise, Boojum, Broomstick, Artful, Wonder, and Upset.[4] Other Whitney horses, according to *The Blood-Horse*, were Tanya, Burgomaster, Iron Mask, Dominant, Daisy F., Jersey Lightning, Barneget, Thunderer, Vivid, Stamina, Borrow, Chicle, Cudgel, Johren, Vexatious, Dr. Clark, John P. Grier, Prudery, Tryster, Whiskaway, Jolly Roger, Mother Goose, Maud Muller, Whiskery, Victorian, Dice, and Diavolo.[5]

In 1914, the two-year-old Regret came in first in each of her three starts. Regret, ridden by jockey Joe Notter, went on to win the 1915 Kentucky Derby. In 1916, the four-year-old filly had the only extreme disappointment of her racing career: she finished absolutely last in the first of two races for that season. Undaunted, she won the second race. In her four 1917 races, Regret won three and placed in one.[6] To date, Regret is the only filly ever to win the Kentucky Derby.

Between 1929 and 1930, a series of events affected the operations of Brookdale Farm and Greentree Stables. The death of James Rowe, Sr., in the autumn of 1929 had left Brookdale Stable without a trainer; Jimmy Rowe, Jr., and Marshall Lilly substituted. Harry Payne Whitney had secured the services of trainer Thomas J. Healey, who had been employed by the late Richard Wilson, president and owner of Saratoga Race Track in New York. Although Harry Payne Whitney died in October, 1930, Healey did come to Brookdale as head trainer in January, 1931. Jimmy Rowe became head trainer at Greentree Stables, with Wilfred Mullin and Marshall Lilly as his assistants.[7]

With the termination of the 1932 Thompson-Whitney contract and the death of Payne Whitney in 1933, Greentree Stables used its own facilities exclusively, under the direction of Mrs. Payne Whitney and their son John Hay (Jock) Whitney. Mrs. Whitney was "known among sportsmen as the

[3] Wilfred Mullin, interview at Lincroft, November 4, 1976.

[4] Elisabeth Thompson Babcock, letter to Philip C. Carling, August 31, 1976.

[5] *The Blood-Horse*, pp. 267-268.

[6] Ibid., p. 268.

[7] ". . . Resident of Red Bank," New York *Herald Tribune*, 26 March 1936.

'First Lady of the Turf.'"[8] Two Kentucky Derby winners, Twenty Grand in 1931 and Shut Out in 1942, were trained at Greentree.[9]

Later, the Greentree Stables relocated in Kentucky under the ownership of John Hay Whitney, former Ambassador to the Court of St. James and formerly Publisher of the New York *Herald Tribune*, and his sister, the late Mrs. (Joan) Charles S. Payson, owner of the Manhasset Stable and the New York Mets.[10] The Greentree Stables establishment in Lincroft was sold in 1947 to Mrs. Alice Sherman Fiorita[11] who, in January 1950, sold the property to Charles Holsey and his son Joseph Holsey.[12] In 1959, the Holsey's Jay Cee Farm of 157 acres was sold to the Brothers of the Christian Schools.[13]

APPENDIX VII: The Thompson Children

Elisabeth Thompson Babcock is the only surviving child of Lewis and Geraldine Thompson. An author and illustrator, Mrs. Babcock was an elected school trustee for forty-seven years. During these years, she was also president of the Board of Education, Common School District Number Thirteen, Township of Oyster Bay, for twenty years, and vice-president of the Board of Education, Central School District Number Two, Syosset, New York, for fifteen years. Among the many citations bestowed upon her are the New York Public Library award, 1949, the New York State Teachers Award, 1949, and the Distinguished Service Award from the New York State School Boards Association, 1969.[1] She holds memberships in the National Forest Association, the American Museum of Natural History, and the National Audubon Society. Married to Richard Franklin Babcock on February 7, 1920, she has four children: Betsy, Geraldine, Alice Woodward, and Anne.

Mrs. Babcock reminisces about her older brother, *William*, and her younger sister, *Geraldine*:

[8] Amy Porter, Asbury Park *Press*, 3 January 1943.

[9] Willie Ratner, "Greentree Farm Now to Be a Breeding Center," Newark *Evening News*, 20 December 1949

[10] William Barclay Harding, "Geraldine Thompson—Lifetime of Dedication and Service," *Daily Register*, 26 January 1965.

[11] Ratner, "Old Greentree Farm Sold," Newark *Evening News*, n. d.

[12] Ratner, "Punching the Bag," Newark *Evening News*, 10 November 1950.

[13] "Christian Brothers Take Title to School Property," Asbury Park *Press*, 8 April 1959.

[1] Who's Who, Inc., "Babcock, Mrs. E. T. (Betty Babcock)," *Who's Who in the East, 1972-1973* (Chicago: Marquis Publications, 1974), p. 28.

. . . . I had driven all night to reach Katonah, New York, where my brother Bill [Dr. William Payne Thompson II] had died. A post mortem was in progress. The cause of death, "an ulcer the size of a grapefruit, lodged in the intestinal tract behind the pancreas, which had cut through a main artery." Then the Pathologist added this. "My God, Mrs. Babcock, there is no pain to equal this, nothing in drugs to assuage it, yet he worked to help others. What courage, what unbelievable courage." This was August, 1948, and Mamma, Bill, Lewis, and I already knew our Puss [Geraldine] was dying of tuberculosis.

Bill was born on April 16, 1897, a blue-eyed infant with curly golden hair and a most amiable disposition. At fifteen, in the late afternoon, being at St. Moritz in Switzerland with his parents and his eight-year-old brother, he mentioned to a boy his own age he was going to climb Mt. Blanc. He was found twenty-four hours later by a mountaineer search party, having dropped ninety feet and landed crushed and bleeding on a ledge. The right leg was a mass of fractures, the left leg paralyzed forever. One year and seventy-six operations later he could stand upright again and learned, once more, to walk.

He entered Yale at seventeen, having made up two years in one at school. He and others of his classmates took leaves of absence in his Junior year to train as Naval pilots, then offered themselves to the United States Navy. They were accepted. Bill, because of his crippled legs, was placed in charge of the Naval flying unit which was formed at M.I.T.

The war over, Bill returned to Yale, graduated, and enrolled in the College of Physicians and Surgeons of the Columbia Medical Center, graduating Phi Beta Kappa.

A seventy-seventh operation on his right leg not inclined to heal rapidly, he asked for and received a staff position at the Rockefeller Hospital in China for half a year. Eyes shining on his return he said, "Such incredible luck. On the way out the ship ran into typhoon. The captain was great; he allowed me to be lashed with him on the bridge. We were there forty-eight hours. You never saw such seas. It was beautiful."

He married Margaret Caughey of Glens Falls whose father was the Pastor of the large Episcopal Church. They went to live near Baltimore as Bill wished to take an intensive course in Pathology at John Hopkins for one year. This completed, he felt equipped to accept the Presbyterian-Columbia Medical Center offer to be on its resident medical staff with a laboratory of his own, and to teach students at the College of Physicians and Surgeons.

He and his wife were blessed with three children: Margaret, Dr. William Payne Thompson III (who died two years ago [1975], age forty-six, of cancer, as brave and good as his father), and Gerald Livingston Thompson.[2]

About "Puss" (Geraldine Thompson Van Gerbig Boone), Mrs. Babcock says:

No one could be indifferent to Puss, nor could anyone forget her.

Puss was either deeply loved or heartily disliked—she found it something of a cross to be so sure of the love of her family. Thus this small bundle of fury did her best to enrage

[2]Elisabeth Thompson Babcock, letters to Linda Lott Rizzo, June 7, 1977, and June 15, 1977.

us. She was so pretty. A strawberry and cream complexion, her little head covered with tumbling golden curls, her straight small nose, well-modelled lips, deep-set, expressive violet eyes, fringed with curling eyelashes, produced a picture of a living Raphael cherub. There the likeness ended. This adorable little creature was determined to wage an undying war against authority.

Every generation has its bevy of beautiful women—Puss', fifty-seven years ago, had four. Miss Emery from Cleveland, Miss Altemus from Philadelphia, and Miss Potter and Puss from New York. To my unprejudiced eye, all four were beautiful, but Puss was devastatingly so.

It amused her, but not for long, to dance "The Charleston" all night long and race around on dusty roads in Stutz Bear Cats. Politically Puss was a radical; about religion an unhappy agnostic until the last years of her short, suffering life; warm hearted and instantly generous to those in trouble; courageous and foolhardy, chaste, sober, intelligent, even brilliant.

Starting in childhood as part of defying authority, she invented stories to bamboozle adults, even other children. We were sitting on a small dock on an Adirondack lake when the thirteen-year-old said to the eleven-year-old, "Puss, you must stop lying. You are an awful liar. It is wrong, it is stupid, and it is dangerous."

"It entertains me—so you keep on being the dull goody-goody."

In all those long stays in sanatoriums trying to recover from tuberculosis, Puss' stories became as infectious as the disease. They were invented and told for their maximum shock value; they entertained (some were very funny) or they horrified. Patients thus frightened to death would write to me to save her from returning to her parents' dirt floor, one-cabin shack shared with pigs and chickens, her alcoholic wreck of a mother, her brutish father who beat us all with an axe handle.

By her own personal courage, her total lack of self-pity, she gave courage to others— It had been at the Bellevue Hospital in 1928 when, after ten months of intensive training and passing the mid-wifery course, she had contracted tuberculosis. Thinking it was only a heavy cold she joined the Frontier Nursing Service in Kentucky. Several months later she became so ill she had to return home. In the next twenty-one years, there would be only brief periods when the disease appeared to be arrested.

Towards the end of her gallant life, following her second marriage, my beautiful Puss said to me, "I did not know such a thing as happiness existed. Now that I know, there is so little time, so very little time." [She died in 1949, eleven months after her brother William.] [3]

Lewis Steenrod Thompson, Jr., (nicknamed Pinky), the youngest of the four children, was a 1926 Princeton University graduate and an executive of the Standard Oil Company of New Jersey. During and after World War II,

[3] Babcock, letter to Linda Lott Rizzo, June 7, 1977, and June 15, 1977.

he served with the War Production Board, the Combined Materials and Resources Board, and the Central Intelligence Agency, and in 1960 became special assistant to the Secretary of the Air Force for manpower, personnel, and the Reserve Forces.[4]

Upon his retirement in 1961, Lewis received the Exceptional Service Award from the Department of the Air Force.[5] Lewis and his wife, Miloulie Thomson Thompson, lived together on her Gillionville Plantation, in Albany, Georgia, until he died of cancer on June 11, 1965.[6] There are three children: Bettina (from Lewis' first marriage), Lewis III, and Walter. Lewis' portion of the Brookdale Farm was sold by his widow to the Monmouth County Board of Chosen Freeholders after the death of Mrs. Geraldine Thompson.[7]

[4] "Lewis S. Thompson Dies in Georgia at Sixty-One," obituary, *Daily Register*, 14 June 1965.
[5] Ibid.
[6] Charles B. Harding, interview at Rumson, November 2, 1976.
[7] Babcock, letter to Philip C. Carling, June 30, 1976.

REFERENCE NOTES

PART I: A TRIANGLE OF LAND
Section I: Beginnings

2. *The First People*
1. Franklin Ellis, *History of Monmouth County* (Philadelphia: R. T. Peck and Co., 1885), p. 47.
2. Ibid., p. 5.
3. Ellis, p. 44.
4. Earl Schenck Miers, *Down in Jersey* (New Brunswick: Rutgers University Press, 1973), p. 19.
5. Ibid., p. 9.

3. *Early Claims to the Land*
1. Ellis, p. 62.
2. Ibid.
3. Ibid., p. 371.
4. Ibid., pp. 586-87.
5. John E. Stillwell, M. D., *Historical and Genealogical Miscellany: Early Settlers of New Jersey and Their Descendants* (New York: n.p., 1914; reprint, Baltimore Genealogical Publishing Co., 1970), III, 444.
6. Ellis, p. 545.
7. Ibid., p. 33.
8. James Steen, *History of Christ Church, Shrewsbury, New Jersey (1702-1903)* (Privately printed limited edition. Copy available in Learning Resource Center, Brookdale Community College, Lincroft, New Jersey), p. 3.

4. *Keeping the Faith*
1. Ellis, p. 519.
2. Ibid., p. 579.
3. Steen, p. 16.
4. Dennis P. Ryan, *New Jersey's Loyalists: New Jersey's Revolutionary Experience #20* (Trenton: New Jersey Historical Commission, 1975), p. 9.

5. *Revolution and Division*
1. Ellis, p. 195.
2. Ibid., p. 159.
3. Ibid., p. 226.

6. *Community and Prosperity*
1. John T. Cunningham, *This Is New Jersey: From High Point to Cape May* (New Brunswick: Rutgers University Press, 1953), p. 193.
2. S. Travers Neidlinger, interview at Leonardo, December 9, 1976.
3. Miers, p. 99.
4. Cunningham, p. 195.

PART I: A TRIANGLE OF LAND
Section II: The Birth of Brookdale Farm

1. *The Withers Acquisition of Brookdale Farm*
    1. Monmouth County Hall of Records, Freehold, New Jersey, Deed Book 241, p. 224.
    2. Hall of Records, Deed Book 279, p. 430.
    3. Hall of Records, Deed Book 313, p. 21.
    4. Hall of Records, Deed Book 405, p. 122.
    5. Ibid., pp. 133-35.
    6. Hall of Records, Deed Book 430, p. 257.
    7. Hall of Records, Deed Book C, p. 140; Deed Book B, p. 17; Deed Book E, pp. 203, 114, 113, 348; Deed Book G, p. 149; Deed Book D, p. 72.

2. *"The Sage of Brookdale"*
    1. W. S. Vosburgh, *Horse Racing in America 1866-1921* (New York: The Scribner Press, 1922), p. 8.
    2. "A Great Turfman Gone," New York *Times*, 19 February 1892.
    3. Ibid.
    4. Ellis, p. 892.
    5. Ibid.
    6. Hall of Records, Deed Book T-3, p. 507.
    7. "A Great Turfman Gone."
    8. Vosburgh, p. 8.
    9. Ibid.
   10. "A Great Turfman Gone."
   11. Ibid.
   12. Hall of Records, Deed Book 3570, p. 723.

PART II: SEVENTY-FIVE YEARS ON BROOKDALE FARM
Section I: The Thompson Era

1. *The Sporting Life*
    1. "Obituary Record: Colonel William P. Thompson," New York *Times*, 4 February 1896.
    2. "Gossip of the Horsemen," New York *Times*, 3 February 1896.
    3. Elisabeth Thompson Babcock, letter to Philip C. Carling, June 30-July 29, 1976.
    4. ". . . Resident of Red Bank," New York *Herald Tribune*, 26 March 1936.

2. *Geraldine Thompson: Spirited from the Start*
    1. Babcock, interview conducted by P. C. Carling, at Woodbury, Long Island, New York, August 25, 1976.
    2. Ibid.
    3. "Mrs. Thompson Once Played Ball Against FDR," Long Branch *Daily Record*, 14 June 1951.
    4. Babcock interview.
    5. Ibid.

6. "Mrs. Lewis S. Thompson Tells of Her Busy Life and Multiple Activities," Long Branch *Daily Record*, 18 August 1940.

3. Wife, Mother, Mistress of Brookdale
1. Laura Harding, interview at Holmdel, November 9, 1976.
2. Leigh Cook, ". . . Had Glamorous Aura," Asbury Park *Press*, 21 April 1974.
3. Babcock, interview at Brookdale Community College, Lincroft, April 25, 1977.
4. Babcock interview.
5. Babcock letter to Mrs. Leigh Cook, Asbury Park *Press*, Asbury Park, March 28-31, 1974.
6. Cook, Asbury Park *Press*.
7. Babcock letter, March 28-31, 1974.
8. Ibid.
9. Ella Kelly Stryker, interview at Lincroft, October 1976.
10. Madelyn Eagen Kelly, interview at Lincroft, October 1976.
11. Ibid.
12. Babcock letter, March 28-31, 1974.
13. Ibid.
14. Ibid.

4. Horses, Brookdale, and the Whitneys
1. ". . . Resident of Red Bank."
2. G. Barker Seeley, "Monmouth Park," *Oceanport in Retrospect*, ed. Borough of Oceanport (New Jersey: Borough of Oceanport, 1970), p. 154.
3. Ibid.
4. William Barclay Harding, "Geraldine Thompson—A Lifetime of Dedication and Service," *Daily Register*, 26 January 1965.
5. Babcock, letter to Dr. Ervin L. Harlacher, December 8, 1971.
6. *The Blood-Horse* (January 17, 1970), p. 267.
7. New York *Sunday Times*, 5 March 1933.
8. Wilfred Mullin, interview at Lincroft, November 4, 1976.
9. Ibid., and telephone conversation with Linda Lott Rizzo, March 23, 1977.

5. Child's Play
1. Stryker interview.
2. Kelly interview.
3. James Walsh, interview at Neptune, December 1, 1976.
4. Babcock, letter to Philip C. Carling, August 31, 1976.
5. Walsh interview.
6. Joan Delehanty and Barbara Niles, interview at Monmouth Beach, November 15, 1976.
7. Ibid.
8. Mullin interview.
9. Kelly interview.
10. Helen O'Neill Grigor, interview at Red Bank, November 9, 1976.
11. Katherine Neuberger, interview at Lincroft, November 30, 1976.
12. Charles B. Harding, interview at Rumson, November 2, 1976.

6. *Educational Concerns*

1. "Mrs. Lewis S. Thompson Tells . . . ." According to a letter to Geraldine L. Thompson, May 6, 1931, from Mabel S. Douglass, Dean of New Jersey College for Women, Mrs. Thompson received an honorary Master of Philanthropy degree from Rutgers University in 1931. An article, "Mrs. Thompson to Get Honorary Doctorate," appearing in the June 13, 1959 Asbury Park *Press* reported that Mrs. Thompson was to receive Monmouth College's first honorary Doctor of Letters degree.
2. L. Harding interview.
3. Mrs. Marshall Lilly, telephone interview, Lincroft, March 23, 1977, and Mullin interview.
4. ". . . Resident of Red Bank."
5. Ibid.
6. Mullin interview.
7. Joseph E. Clayton, interview at West Belmar, December 1, 1976.
8. Babcock letter, June 30-July 29, 1976.

7. *Hither and Yon: Automobiles and Airplanes*

1. L. Harding interview.
2. Ibid.
3. Walsh interview.
4. Delehanty and Niles interview.
5. Stryker interview.
6. Mullin interview.
7. Walsh interview.
8. Mullin interview.
9. Ibid., and telephone interviews, Lincroft, March 23, 1977, and July 28, 1977.
10. Matthew J. Gill, "Mullin's Lincroft Memories: What the Thompsons Didn't Own Whitneys Did," *Courier*, 11 November 1976.
11. Ibid.
12. ". . . Resident of Red Bank."

8. *Family Life*

1. Babcock interview.
2. Eleanor Marko, "Mrs. Thompson's Day of Recollection: Grand Lady of Brookdale Turns Ninety-Five," *Daily Register*, 4 March 1967.
3. Babcock, letter to Linda Lott Rizzo, July 21, 1977.
4. Stryker interview.
5. ". . . Resident of Red Bank."
6. W. B. Harding, "Geraldine Thompson—A Lifetime . . . ."
7. Stryker interview.
8. ". . . Resident of Red Bank."
9. Ibid.
10. Ibid.
11. "Profile: Mrs. Thompson of Brookdale Farm," *Welfare Reporter* (New Jersey Department of Institutions and Agencies, June 1950), p.6.
12. ". . . Resident of Red Bank."
13. Stryker interview.
14. Babcock interview.

15. Babcock interview.
16. Stryker interview.
17. L. Harding interview.
18. Babcock, "Brookdale Farm . . . ," *Lewis Steenrod and Geraldine Livingston Thompson Park*, ed. Monmouth County Park System (New Jersey: Monmouth County Park System), p. 3.

9. *The Village*
1. Mullin interview.
2. Gill, "What the Thompsons Didn't . . . ."
3. Ibid.
4. Mullin interview.
5. Gill, "What the Thompsons Didn't . . . ."
6. W. Gilbert Manson, interview at Middletown, November 11, 1976.
7. Gill, "What the Thompsons Didn't . . . ."
8. Babcock letter, July 21, 1977.

10. *Changes*
1. Babcock letter, August 31, 1976.
2. Mullin interview.
3. Babcock, "Brookdale Farm . . . ."
4. Babcock, telephone interview, Woodbury, New York, August 10, 1977.
5. Jack Mehl, "Five-Hundred Acre Brookdale Farms to Continue Housing Families," *Sunday Call,* 21 April 1946.
6. Freehold *Transcript,* 22 January 1953.
7. Mehl, "Five-Hundred Acre Brookdale Farms . . . ."

PART II: SEVENTY-FIVE YEARS ON BROOKDALE FARM
Section II: The Great Lady of Brookdale

1. *Profile: Geraldine Livingston Thompson*
1. Elisabeth T. Babcock, letter to Leigh Cook, March 28-31, 1974.
2. Babcock, letter to Philip C. Carling, received August 31, 1976.
3. Beatrice O. Freeman, "My Most Unforgettable Character," draft of an article, n. d., Geraldine L. Thompson personal file.
4. Ibid.
5. Ibid.

2. *An Unpopular Cause*
1. Former State Senator Richard R. Stout, interview at Allenhurst, November 1, 1976.
2. State Senator Alfred N. Beadleston, interview at Red Bank, November 23, 1976.
3. Laura Harding, interview at Holmdel, November 9, 1976.
4. Babcock, interview with Philip C. Carling, Woodbury, New York, August 25, 1976.
5. Former United States Ambassador Katharine Elkus White, interview at Red Bank, October 12, 1976.
6. Katherine Neuberger, interview at Lincroft, November 30, 1976.

3. *An Ardent Churchwoman*

   1. White interview.
   2. Babcock, letter to Leigh Cook.
   3. Neuberger interview.
   4. L. Harding interview.

4. Practicality
   1. Babcock, letter to Leigh Cook.
   2. Freeman.
   3. *Daily Register,* 4 March 1967.
   4. White interview.
   5. S. Travers Neidlinger, interview at Leonardo, December 9, 1976.
   6. W. Gilbert Manson, interview at Middletown, November 11, 1976.
   7. L. Harding interview.
   8. White interview.

5. Idealism and Determination
   1. Stout interview.
   2. Ibid.
   3. Freeman.
   4. Charles B. Harding, interview at Rumson, November 2, 1976.
   5. White interview.
   6. Stout interview.
   7. "Jersey Honor Paid to Mrs. Thompson," New York *Times,* 2 June 1950.
   8. Jane Foderaro, "'. . . and Gladly She Lived,' Hundreds Eulogize Mrs. Thompson," *Daily Register,* 8 October 1967.

6. Perseverance
   1. Babcock interview, August 25, 1976.
   2. Bill Placek, "New Jersey's First Citizen Also First Beaver," Long Branch *Daily Record,* 13 June 1951.
   3. Babcock interview, August 25, 1976.
   4. Placek.

7. The Strategist
   1. H. Roemer McPhee, letter to Richard H. Pough, April 30, 1951.
   2. Ibid.
   3. Geraldine L. Thompson, letter to Geoffrey Parsons, June 1, 1951.
   4. Thompson, letter to "Helen," of the New York *Herald Tribune,* July 3, 1953.
   5. Richard H. Pough, letter to Geraldine L. Thompson, March 29, 1951.
   6. "Phipps State Park," editorial, New York *Herald Tribune,* June 23, 1953.
   7. Thompson, letter to "Helen."

8. Recruiter of the Young
   1. Beadleston interview.
   2. L. Harding interview.
   3. Ibid.
   4. Stout interview.
   5. Neuberger interview.

9. *Humor*
   1. L. Harding interview.
   2. Ibid.
   3. C. B. Harding interview.
   4. Stout interview.

10. *Punctual, Prepared, and Ever Gracious*
   1. Babcock, note attached to draft of speech delivered by Geraldine L. Thompson at Stacy-Trent Hotel, Trenton, May 17, 1957, Geraldine L. Thompson personal file.
   2. Neidlinger interview.
   3. "Mrs. Lewis S. Thompson Tells . . . ."
   4. Beadleston interview.
   5. Stout interview.

11. *Public Health and Welfare*
   1. "Promoter of Welfare," *Welfare Reporter,* August 1946, p. 3.
   2. Draft of an article on Monmouth County Organization for Social Service (MCOSS) for *Welfare Reporter,* 19 October 1967, Geraldine L. Thompson personal file.
   3. Ibid.
   4. "Tribute to Mrs. Lewis Thompson," Red Bank *Register,* 19 July 1951.
   5. "Dedication Honors Geraldine Thompson," Asbury Park *Press,* 21 October 1957.
   6. "How the MCOSS Grew . . . ," *Welfare Reporter,* May 1950, p. 4.
   7. Ibid.
   8. "Mrs. Thompson to Step Down as President of Social Services," Asbury Park *Press,* 20 November 1952.
   9. Eleanor Roosevelt, "Showing the Way," New York *World Telegram,* 5 October 1946.
   10. "How the MCOSS Grew."
   11. "Mrs. Thompson to Lay Cornerstone," Long Branch *Daily Record,* 23 December 1931.
   12. "How the MCOSS Grew."
   13. Ibid.
   14. "Groups Join in Handling of Health Problems," Red Bank *Register,* 15 May 1947.
   15. Dr. Joseph E. Clayton, member of Board of Trustees, Brookdale Community College, interview at West Belmar, December 1, 1976.
   16. "MCOSS Home Is Dedicated," Red Bank *Register,* 8 June 1950.
   17. MCOSS Family Health and Nursing Service, *National League for Nursing Accreditation Report,* June 24, 1976.
   18. Winifred Livengood, Executive Director, Home Health Agency Assembly of New Jersey, Inc., letter to Meline Karakashian, July 22, 1977.

12. *Juvenile Justice and Prison Reform*
   1. "Mrs. Thompson to Step Down . . . ."
   2. "Mrs. Lewis S. Thompson Tells . . . ."
   3. "Mrs. Thompson, 89 Today, Feted on Visit to County Jail," Asbury Park *Press,* 2 March 1961.
   4. "Mrs. Thompson Remembered by Scores on 88th Birthday," Asbury Park *Press,* 6 March 1960.

5. "Mrs. Thompson Shakes Off Hurts: She Is Back on a Busy Schedule," Asbury Park *Press,* 18 January 1955.
6. "Mrs. Thompson Remembered."
7. Ibid.
8. Ibid.
9. "Mrs. Roosevelt Suggests State Revaluate Education Program," Asbury Park *Press,* 4 June 1959.
10. Ibid.
11. Ibid.
12. Charles W. Houston, letter to Geraldine L. Thompson, June 13, 1963.
13. L. Harding interview.
14. Thompson, letter to Mrs. Lewis W. Jones, December 10, 1952.
15. "Mrs. Thompson Founds New Scholarship Fund," Asbury Park *Press,* 4 February 1965.
16. "State Institutions Board to Honor Mrs. Thompson, " Asbury Park *Press,* 2 May 1957.
17. "Mrs. Thompson Asks Goal for Humanity," Asbury Park *Press,* 2 March 1962.
18. Thompson, letter to Commissioner John Tramburg, November 6, 1959.
19. Thompson, letter to Lloyd Wescott, May 16, 1961.
20. "Clinton Holds Graduation in Mrs. Thompson's Honor," *Welfare Reporter,* May 1957.
21. Babcock, note attached to draft of speech. . . .
22. Thompson, draft of a speech, May 17, 1957, Geraldine L. Thompson personal file.

13. *Liberation, Women and Politics*
1. Neuberger interview.
2. Emma Bugbee, "Committeewoman Tells Why Dishonest Politics Made Her Resign," New York *Herald Tribune,* 23 October 1927.
3. Thompson, "Women in Politics," draft of an address, June 2, 1931, Geraldine L. Thompson personal file.
4. Ibid.
5. Bugbee.
6. Ibid.
7. "Geraldine L. Thompson Dies: Social Worker and G.O.P. Aide," New York *Times,* 10 September 1967.
8. Ibid.
9. "Politics, Parks: Mrs. Thompson Shares Thoughts," *Daily Register,* 9 January 1931.
10. "High Tribute Is Paid to Mrs. G. L. Thompson," Asbury Park *Press,* 4 May 1931.
11. Placek.
12. "Geraldine L. Thompson Dies."
13. Thompson, "Women in Politics."
14. Bugbee.
15. "Mrs. G. L. Thompson 'Harmony' Leader," Asbury Park *Press,* 23 June 1931.
16. "Pioneer Welfare Worker, Mrs. Thompson, Dies at 95," Asbury Park *Press,* 10 September 1967.

14. *Democracy and the Two Party System*
1. W. B. Harding.

2. White interview.
3. Babcock, letter to Linda Lott Rizzo, July 21, 1977.
4. "Tolerance in Politics Discussed by Women," Newark *Evening News,* 7 March 1931.
5. "Mrs. Thompson Hostess to 400 Leaders of County," n.p., 7 May 1931, Geraldine L. Thompson personal file.

15. *Nature, Children, and Scouting*
1. "Mrs. Thompson Says She'll Give County Estate as Children's Park," Asbury Park *Press,* 1 March 1964.
2. Placek, "Mrs. Thompson Once Played Ball Against FDR," Long Branch *Daily Record,* 14 June 1951.
3. "Color Bird Chart Offered to Clubs," Oklahoma City *Oklahoman,* 2 March 1958.
4. Shirley Miller, National Audubon Society, postcard to Geraldine L. Thompson, n.d., Geraldine L. Thompson personal file.
5. "Character Always Counts," *Courier,* 5 April 1962.
6. "Museum Showing Wildlife of City," New York *Times,* 25 January 1954.
7. Babcock, note attached to *National Geographic*'s special issue on the American Museum of Natural History, n.d., Geraldine L. Thompson personal file.
8. C. B. Harding, letter to Mrs. Lewis S. Thompson, December 6, 1963.
9. C. B. Harding, letter to Mrs. Lewis S. Thompson, November 13, 1963.
10. "County Boy Scouts Mark Anniversary," n.p., n.d. (1965), Geraldine L. Thompson personal file.
11. Placek.
12. "Scout Party," Asbury Park *Press,* 16 February 1955.
13. "Ancient Mariner Thompson," *Congressional Record,* May 19, 1954.
14. "Boy Scout Camp to Be Named in Honor of Mrs. Thompson," Asbury Park *Press,* 9 February 1958.
15. "Mrs. Thompson Feted for Aid to Girl Scouts," Asbury Park *Press,* 2 July 1964.

16. *Education: Assistance Given and Honors Received*
1. Thompson, letter to Carl A. Sheridan, August 15, 1952.
2. "Shore Woman Pays for Study Journey," Asbury Park *Press,* 22 August 1955.
3. Thompson, letter to Commissioner Tramburg.
4. "New School Named for Mrs. Thompson," Asbury Park *Press,* 26 May 1962.
5. "Mrs. Thompson Gets Degree at Jersey College," New York *Herald Tribune,* 6 June 1931.
6. Thompson, letter to Dean Mabel S. Douglass, May 7, 1931.
7. "Mrs. Thompson, 89 Today . . . ."
8. "Mrs. Thompson to Get Honorary Doctorate," Asbury Park *Press,* 13 June 1959.

17. *Planning the Future of Brookdale*
1. Thompson, letter to Commissioner Tramburg.
2. E. Donald Sterner, telephone interview, Belmar, March 17, 1977.
3. Sterner, interview at Belmar, January 26, 1977.
4. Ira Henry Freeman, "Jersey Hails Social Worker, 88, Who Is Only Technically Retired," New York *Times,* 2 March 1960.
5. "200 at Surprise Fete for Mrs. Thompson," Asbury Park *Press,* 3 March 1952.
6. "Politics, Parks: Mrs. Thompson Shares Thoughts."

7. "Mrs. Thompson Says She'll Give County Estate . . . ."
8. "Freeholders to Plan Thompson Park," Asbury Park *Press,* 1 October 1967.

18. *"And Gladly She Lived"*
1. Foderaro.
2. Freeman.
3. Babcock, letter to P. C. Carling received August 31, 1976.
4. Freeman.
5. Foderaro.
6. White interview.

PART III: BROOKDALE COMMUNITY COLLEGE
Section I: The Founding

1. A College to Be Proud Of
1. Katherine Neuberger, Chairman of New Jersey Board of Higher Education, interview at Lincroft, November 30, 1976.
2. William O. Fleckenstein, Trustee, Brookdale Community College, interview at Holmdel, January 25, 1977.
3. Major General W. Preston Corderman, former Chairman, Board of Trustees, Brookdale Community College, interview at Little Silver, November 23, 1976.
4. Leon Zuckerman, Trustee, Brookdale Community College, interview at Middletown, September 15, 1976.

2. Of The People
1. James R. Greene, former Trustee, Brookdale Community College, interview at Fair Haven, January 8, 1977.
2. Ibid.
3. New Jersey State Department of Education, *Education Beyond High School: The Two-Year Community College,* a report of the New Jersey State Board of Education to the governor and the legislature (Trenton: January, 1961), p. 13.
4. New Jersey State Department of Education, *Higher Education in New Jersey, 1945-67: An Accounting by the State Board of Education of Its Stewardship of Higher Education* (Trenton: July, 1967), p. 23.
5. New Jersey State Department of Education, *Education Beyond High School.*
6. Ibid.
7. Ibid., p. 4.
8. Ibid., p. 45.
9. Ibid., p. 13.
10. Dr. Joseph E. Clayton, Trustee, Brookdale Community College, interview at West Belmar, December 1, 1976.
11. Ibid.
12. Ibid.
13. Ibid.
14. Joseph C. Irwin, former Director, Monmouth County Board of Chosen Freeholders, interview at Red Bank, September 20, 1976.
15. The Study Committee, *A Study of the Need for a Two-Year County College in*

Monmouth County, presented to the Monmouth County Board of Chosen Free-holders, Freehold, December 1965, p. 5.

3. *The Law's Delay*

1. State Senator Alfred N. Beadleston, interview at Red Bank, November 23, 1976.
2. The Study Committee, p. 1.
3. Ibid., p. 7.
4. Ibid.
5. Earl B. Garrison, former Trustee, Brookdale Community College, interview held at Freehold, September 2, 1976.
6. "College Study Unit Finishes Report Draft," Asbury Park *Press,* 28 September 1965.
7. "College Report Given to Board," Asbury Park *Press,* 19 December 1965.
8. Paul Zar, interview at Red Bank, December 9, 1976.
9. Irwin interview.
10. Mike Ward, "Ground Zero," *Advisor,* 28 October 1970.
11. Zar interview.
12. Elisabeth A. Kelley, interview at Lincroft, October 26, 1976.
13. Audrie LaTowsky, former County College Study Committee Chairman, Northern Monmouth County Branch of the American Association of University Women, and past Vice-Chairman of Board of Trustees, Brookdale Community College, interview at Wyckoff, N. J., August 11, 1976.
14. Ibid.
15. Ibid.
16. Mary Lou Wagner, former President, Northern Monmouth County Branch of the American Association of University Women, interview at Lincroft, December 8, 1976.
17. Northern Monmouth County Branch of the American Association of University Women, *Minutes of the Board of Directors,* May 25, 1965.
18. "University Women Demand Results of College Study, Threaten Action," Asbury Park *Press,* 6 June 1965.
19. LaTowsky interview, August 11, 1976.
20. Ibid.
21. Audrie LaTowsky, *County College Study Committee Report,* May, 1966, pp. 1, 2.
22. Garrison interview.
23. Ibid.
24. Zuckerman interview.
25. Dr. Joseph I. Robinson, "The Development of a Community College as a Reflection of Selected Social, Economic, and Political Characteristics of the Community" (D.Ed. dissertation, New York University, 1972), pp. 29, 30.
26. Garrison interview.
27. The Study Committee, p. 14.
28. Ibid.

4. *A Dignity of Its Own*

1. State Senator Eugene J. Bedell, former Monmouth County Freeholder, interview at Keansburg, December 1, 1976.
2. Bedell interview.

3. Irwin interview.
4. Elinor Multer, former education writer, *Daily Register,* interview at Lincroft, July 7, 1975.
5. Audrie LaTowsky, *Report on County Colleges,* address given to Monmouth County Council, League of Women Voters, Red Bank, March 31, 1966, pp. 6, 7.
6. LaTowsky interview, August 11, 1976.
7. Irwin interview.
8. Monmouth County Council, League of Women Voters, untitled press release, February 3, 1967, personal file of Mrs. Josephine Lee, Red Bank.
9. Mrs. Kenneth M. Mitchell, former President, Monmouth County Council, League of Women Voters, letter to Monmouth County Board of Chosen Freeholders, March 17, 1967, personal file of Mrs. Josephine Lee, Red Bank.
10. Bedell interview.
11. LaTowsky interview.
12. Garrison interview.
13. "Freeholders Find Few Against Monmouth County College Idea," Asbury Park *Press,* 5 April 1967.
14. Multer interview.
15. Carolyn Nilson, former President, Northern Monmouth County Branch of the American Association of University Women, letter to Joan Grantges, December 19, 1976.
16. Anita Bellin, interview at Middletown, November 29, 1976.

5. *The Turning of the Tide*
1. Irwin interview.
2. Bellin interview.
3. Ibid.
4. Benjamin H. Danskin, former Monmouth County Freeholder, interview at Wall Township, December 17, 1976.
5. Irwin interview.
6. LaTowsky interview, August 11, 1976.
7. Irwin interview.
8. Ibid.
9. Garrison interview.
10. Robinson, p. 51.
11. LaTowsky interview, August 11, 1976.
12. Beadleston interview.

6. *Nothing Succeeds Like Success*
1. Irwin interview.
2. Bellin interview.
3. Zar interview.
4. Dr. Ervin L. Harlacher, first President of Brookdale Community College, letter to Mary Lou Wagner, October 10, 1969.

7. *The Ideal Location: A Triangle of Land*
1. Danskin interview.
2. Ibid.

8. For the People
1. Bellin interview.
2. Ibid.
3. Monmouth County Council, League of Women Voters, *Statement Regarding Quali-fications of Board of Trustees for Proposed Community College,* April, 1967, file of Mrs. Josephine Lee, Red Bank.
4. Arthur Z. Kamin, editor, *Daily Register,* interview at Shrewsbury, December 10, 1976.
5. LaTowsky interview, August 11, 1976.
6. Nilson.
7. Carolyn Nilson, letter to Joan Grantges, December 19, 1976.
8. Bellin interview.
9. Bedell interview.
10. Danskin interview.
11. LaTowsky interview, August 11, 1976.
12. Irwin interview.
13. Ibid.

PART III: BROOKDALE COMMUNITY COLLEGE
Section II: The Impossible Dream

1. The Impossible Dream
1. "9.3 Million College Budget Set," *Daily Register,* 14 November 1967.
2. Corderman interview.
3. Marvin A. Clark, former Trustee, Brookdale Community College, interview at Free-hold, November 11, 1976.
4. Garrison interview.
5. Clark interview.
6. Zuckerman interview.
7. Fleckenstein interview.
8. Zuckerman interview.
9. Clark interview.
10. Harlacher, speakerphone interview between Lincroft and Kansas City, Missouri, January 25, 1977.
11. Ibid.
12. Ibid.
13. Zuckerman interview.
14. Audrie LaTowsky, former Trustee, Brookdale Community College, interview in Middletown, November 2, 1976.
15. LaTowsky interview, August 11, 1976.
16. Corderman interview.
17. LaTowsky interview, November 2, 1976.
18. Harlacher interview.
19. Zuckerman interview.
20. LaTowsky interview, August 11, 1976.
21. Harlacher interview.
22. "New College Leader Outlines His Policies," *Daily Register,* 8 March 1968.

23. Edith Reilly, Executive Assistant and Secretary to the Board of Trustees, Brookdale Community College, interview in Lincroft, December 9, 1976.
24. Myrna Gray, "Focus on Education: County College May Adopt New Concept," Asbury Park *Sunday Press,* 7 April 1968.
25. Corderman interview.
26. Fleckenstein interview.
27. Joe King, "You Can't Tell Brookdale By Its Cover," Woodbridge *News-Tribune,* 8 June 1972.
28. Elinor Ebeling, Dean of the Learning Resources Center, Brookdale Community College, interview at Lincroft, December 2, 1976.
29. Editorial, Asbury Park *Press,* 8 July, 1968.
30. Danskin interview.
31. Ibid.
32. Thomas H. Auch, Vice President and Treasurer, Brookdale Community College, interview at Lincroft with Thomas H. Auch and Shirley Zeisel, former Administrative Assistant, Brookdale Community College, November 17, 1976.
33. Ibid.
34. Ibid.
35. LaTowsky interview, November 2, 1976.
36. Zuckerman interview.
37. Corderman interview.
38. Clark interview.
39. Reilly interview.
40. Shirley Zeisel, Auch and Zeisel interview.
41. Reilly interview.
42. Corderman interview.
43. Multer interview.
44. "Mrs. Multer Gets Post at Brookdale Community College," *Daily Register,* September, 1968.
45. Thomas H. Auch, Auch and Zeisel interview.
46. LaTowsky interview, November 2, 1976.
47. Multer interview.
48. Zuckerman interview.
49. Harlacher interview.
50. Zuckerman interview.
51. Bernard Kellenyi, Architect of Brookdale Community College, interview at Red Bank, November 9, 1976.
52. Danskin interview.

3. *The College Without Walls*

1. Donald P. Hoagland, Superintendent of the Monmouth County Vocational School District, interview at West Long Branch, December 1, 1976.
2. Fred B. Hazlett, first Director of Admissions, Brookdale Community College, interview at Lincroft, October 26, 1976.
3. Ervin L. Harlacher, *Five Years Ahead of the Future: The President's Report to the Board of Trustees* (Lincroft: Brookdale Community College, 1973) pp. 3-5.
4. Kellenyi interview.
5. Thomas H. Auch, Auch and Zeisel interview.

6. Shirley Zeisel, Auch and Zeisel interview.
7. Kellenyi interview.
8. Clark interview.
9. Kellenyi interview.
10. Ibid.
11. Charles L. Morgan, first Legal Counsel, Brookdale Community College, interview at Long Branch, October 28, 1976.
12. Harlacher interview.
13. LaTowsky interview, November 2, 1976.
14. Martha Thompson, Media Specialist, Brookdale Community College, interview at Lincroft, October 20, 1976.
15. Linda Ellis, "College Keeps Its Old Barn Appeal," Newark *Evening News,* 3 October 1969.
16. Irwin interview.
17. Harlacher interview.
18. Lucille Lubow, member of first graduating class, Brookdale Community College, interview at Lincroft, November 10, 1976.
19. Karl Fox, member of first graduating class, Brookdale Community College, interview at Lincroft, November 9, 1976.
20. Anita Clax, member of first graduating class, Brookdale Community College, interview at Lincroft, November 1, 1976.
21. Ibid.
22. Fox interview.
23. Clax interview.
24. Ebeling interview.
25. Harlacher interview.
26. Fox interview.
27. Ibid.
28. Thomas H. Auch, Auch and Zeisel interview.
29. Fox interview.
30. Jacqueline Alban, "200 Students At Brookdale Vote Class Boycott Protest," Asbury Park *Press,* 7 May 1970.
31. Doris Kulman, "Brookdale Groups Form Coalition," *Daily Register,* 13 May 1970.
32. Ibid.
33. Kellenyi interview.
34. Robert W. Leonard, interview at Lincroft, December 16, 1976.
35. Fox interview.
36. Editorial, *Daily Register,* 8 July 1970.
37. Lubow interview.
38. Lubow interview.
39. "Brookdale Education Plan Seen Successful," *Daily Register,* 22 September 1971.
40. Clayton interview.
41. Kellenyi interview.
42. Doris Kulman, "Brookdale Buildings Impress Visitors," *Daily Register,* 22 September 1971.
43. Thomas H. Auch, Auch and Zeisel interview.
44. Reilly interview.
45. Wagner interview.

BIBLIOGRAPHY

BOOKS

Beck, Henry Charlton. *Fare to Midlands.* New York: E. P. Dutton and Co., Inc., 1949.

Cunningham, John T. *This Is New Jersey from High Point to Cape May.* New Brunswick: Rutgers University Press, 1953.

Ellis, Franklin. *History of Monmouth County, New Jersey.* Philadelphia: R. T. Peck and Co., 1885.

Horner, William G. *This Old Monmouth of Ours.* Freehold: Moreau Brothers, 1932. Reprint, Allenhurst, New Jersey, under patronage of Morris Genealogical Library, 1974.

Lash, Joseph P. *Eleanor: The Years Alone.* New York: W. W. and Co., Inc., 1972.

Mandeville, Ernest W. *The Story of Middletown, the Oldest Settlement in New Jersey.* Middletown: Christ Church, 1972.

McMahon, T. J. *The Golden Age of the Monmouth County Shore: 1864-1914.* Fair Haven: T. J. McMahon, 1964.

Miers, Earl Schenck. *Down in Jersey.* New Brunswick: Rutgers University Press, 1973.

President's Commission on National Goals. *Goals for Americans.* New York: Prentice-Hall, 1960.

Salter, Edwin. *History of Monmouth and Ocean Counties.* Bayonne, New Jersey: E. Gardner and Son, 1890.

Smith, Goldwin. *A History of England.* New York: Charles Scribner's Sons, 1949.

Steen, James. *History of Christ Church, Shrewsbury, New Jersey (1702-1903).* Privately printed limited ed., n.d.

Stillwell, John E., M.D. *Historical and Genealogical Miscellany: Early Settlers of New Jersey and Their Descendants.* Vol. III. New York: n.p., 1914. Reprint, Baltimore Genealogical Publishing Co., 1970.

Vosburgh, W. S. *Horse Racing in America, 1866-1921.* New York: The Scribner Press, 1922.

Who's Who, Inc. "Babcock, Mrs. E. T." *Who's Who in the East, 1972-73.* Chicago: Marquis Publications, 1974.

DOCUMENTS

Brookdale Community College. *Founder's Day.* October 17, 1971.

Carlin, Elizabeth. Draft of an article on MCOSS for the *Welfare Reporter,* October 19, 1967. Geraldine L. Thompson personal file.

Christ Church, Shrewsbury. *Recorded Deeds.* N.d.

Christ Episcopal Church, Middletown. *In Memoriam: Geraldine Livingston Thompson, March 2, 1872-September 7, 1967,* October 8, 1967.

Cody, Edward J. *Religious Issue in Revolutionary New Jersey.* New Jersey Historical Commission, 1975.

Fenton, Carol Lane. *New Jersey's Geological Past.* Trenton: New Jersey State Museum, September 4, 1962.

Ferrell, Dr. Guy V., Director. *A Study of the Proposal to Establish and Operate a County College in Monmouth County: Report of the Commissioner of Education to the New*

212

Jersey State Board of Education. Trenton: State Department of Education, October, 1966.

Freeman, Beatrice O. "My Most Unforgettable Character," draft of an article, n.d., Geraldine L. Thompson personal file.

Harlacher, Dr. Ervin L. *Five Years Ahead of the Future: President's Report to the Board of Trustees, 1968-1973.* Brookdale Community College.

Historical Committee of Colts Neck. *History of Colts Neck.* N.d.

LaTowsky, Audrie. *County College Study Committee Report, 1966.* Northern Monmouth County Branch of the American Association of University Women, branch files.

League of Women Voters of Red Bank Area. *Bulletin.* March, 1966; January, 1967.

Monmouth County Council, League of Women Voters. *Statement Regarding Qualifications of Board of Trustees for Proposed County College,* April, 1967. Personal file of Mrs. Josephine Lee, Red Bank.

———. Untitled press release, February 3, 1967. Personal file of Mrs. Josephine Lee, Red Bank.

Monmouth County Environmental Council. *Natural Features Study for Monmouth County,* April, 1975.

Monmouth County Hall of Records. *Recorded Deeds, 1680-1968.*

Monmouth County Organization for Social Service (MCOSS) Family Health and Nursing Service. *National League for Nursing Accreditation Report.* June 24, 1976.

Monmouth County Park System. *Lewis Steenrod and Geraldine Livingston Thompson Park.* N.d.

Monmouth Park Jockey Club Publicity Department. *Monmouth Park: From Mauve to Modern.* 1956.

Nilson, Carolyn. Untitled record of AAUW College Study Committee meeting with Freeholder Director Irwin, September 25, 1967. Northern Monmouth County Branch of the American Association of University Women, branch files.

New Jersey State Department of Education. *Education Beyond High School: The Two-Year Community College,* a report of the New Jersey State Board of Education to the governor and the legislature. Trenton: January, 1961.

———. *Higher Education in New Jersey, 1945-1967: An Accounting by the State Board of Education of Its Stewardship of Higher Education.* Trenton: July, 1967.

Northern Monmouth County Branch of the American Association of University Women, *Minutes of the Board of Directors' Meetings.* May 25, 1965.

Robinson, Dr. Joseph I. *"The Development of a Community College as a Reflection of Selected Social, Economic, and Political Characteristics of the Community."* D.Ed. Dissertation, New York University, 1972.

Ryan, Dennis P. *New Jersey's Loyalists.* New Jersey Historical Commission, 1975.

Seeley, G. Barker, "Monmouth Park," *Oceanport in Retrospect.* Borough of Oceanport, 1970.

Strayer, George D. *Needs of New Jersey in Higher Education, 1962-1970: A Study Prepared for the State Board of Education.* Trenton: State Department of Education, April, 1962.

Study Committee. *A Study of the Need for a Two-Year County College in Monmouth County.* Presented to the Monmouth County Board of Chosen Freeholders, December, 1965.

Thompson, Mrs. Lewis S. *History of Allenwood Sanatorium, the Tuberculosis Hospital of Monmouth County.* N.p., c. 1928.

———. Drafts of speech delivered at Stacy-Trent Hotel, Trenton, May 17, 1957. Geraldine L. Thompson personal file.

———. "Women in Politics." Draft of a speech, June 2, 1931. Geraldine L. Thompson personal file.

United States Government Printing Office. "Ancient Mariner Thompson." *Congressional Record*. Washington, D. C., May 19, 1954.

Wagner, Mary Lou. *A Voluntary Organization's Involvement in the Establishment of an Educational Institution*. Paper written for History of Education course, Rutgers University Graduate School of Education, March 30, 1976.

MAGAZINES

Blood Horse, 6 November 1948, pp. 312-14.

Newman, Neil. "Top Races of Top Horses—Regret: She Won Other Races Besides the Kentucky Derby." *The Blood Horse*, 20 November 1948, pp. 482, 517.

"New Schools at a Bargain Rate." *Life*, 22 October 1971.

"Regret." *The Blood Horse*, 17 January 1970, pp. 267-68.

Welfare Reporter: New Jersey Department of Institutions and Agencies, August 1946; May 1950; June 1950; July 1950; May 1957; October 1967.

Thoroughbred Record, 1 July 1927, p. 6.

———. 20 November 1915, p. 248.

NEWSPAPERS

Advisor. 28 October 1970.

Asbury Park *Press*. 11 April 1931; 4 May 1931; 20 May 1931; 23 June 1931; 16 September 1935; 25 March 1936; 4 December 1937; 29 December 1937; 3 January 1943; 23 June 1947; 28 February 1948; 4 May 1950; 12 May 1950; 18 May 1950; 2 June 1950; 3 June 1950; 8 December 1950; 8 March 1951; 30 October 1951; 3 March 1952; 4 May 1952; 12 July 1952; 23 July 1952; 20 November 1952; 30 November 1952; 2 May 1954; 16 November 1954; 18 January 1955; 16 February 1955; 22 August 1955; 2 May 1957; 4 May 1957; 17 May 1957; 21 October 1957; 9 February 1958; 22 August 1958; 8 April 1959; 4 June 1959; 13 June 1959; 2 March 1960; 6 March 1960; 2 March 1961; 2 March 1962; 3 March 1962; 13 March 1962; 26 May 1962; 4 January 1964; 1 March 1964; 2 July 1964; 4 February 1965; 10 September 1967; 10 September 1967; 12 September 1967; 1 October 1967; 7 April 1968; 8 July 1968; 7 May 1970; 9 May 1971; 21 April 1974; 13 April 1977.

Atlantic Highlands *Journal*. 1 June 1950.

Camden *Courier-Post*. 3 March 1952.

"County Boy Scouts Mark Anniversary," n.p., n.d., 1965, from Geraldine L. Thompson personal file.

Courier. 5 April 1962; 11 November 1976; 18 November 1976.

Flemington *Democrat*. 26 June 1958.

Freehold *Transcript*. 4 May 1950; 18 May 1950; 22 January 1953.

Jersey Observer. June 1949.

Long Branch *Daily Record*. 15 May 1931; 22 June 1931; 23 December 1931; 16 September 1935; 18 August 1940; 4 May 1950; 2 June 1950; 29 June 1950; 13 June 1951;

14 June 1951; 2 March 1961; 21 September 1961; 26 January 1965.

Matawan *Journal.* 11 May 1950; 8 June 1950.

Monmouth American. 19 May 1950; 22 March 1962.

Monmouth Message. 30 May 1950.

Newark *Evening News.* 7 March 1931; 16 March 1931; 20 December 1949; 2 June 1950;
10 November 1950; 3 October 1969.

New York *Herald Tribune.* 23 October 1927; 6 June 1931; 25 March 1936; 30 May 1950;
4 June 1950; 23 June 1953.

New York *Post.* 9 June 1959.

New York *Times.* 19 February 1892; 3 February 1896; 4 February 1896; 2 June 1930;
5 March 1933; 2 June 1950; 25 January 1954; 25 November 1954; 2 March 1960;
10 September 1967; 23 September 1973.

New York *World-Telegram.* 20 May 1950; 5 October 1946; 15 October 1946.

Ocean County Daily Times. 10 December 1975.

Oklahoma City *Oklahoman.* 2 March 1958.

Passaic *Herald News.* 7 March 1952.

Red Bank *Register* and *Daily Register.* 24 February 1892; 5 February 1896; 22 July
1937; 5 August 1937; 14 November 1935; 8 May 1947; 15 May 1947; 23 September
1948; 1 June 1950; 8 June 1950; 8 June 1950; 19 July 1951; 19 July 1957; 31 July
1952; 30 October 1952; 9 January 1961; 17 March 1961; 9 November 1961;
26 January 1965; 14 June 1965; 4 March 1967; 11 September 1967; 8 October 1967;
9 October 1967; 14 November 1967; n.d. September 1968; 13 May 1970; 8 July 1970;
22 September 1971; 13 October 1971; 6 October 1975.

Shore Record. 14 October 1974.

Spring Lake *Gazette.* 26 June 1947.

Sunday Call. 21 April 1946.

Trenton *Evening Times.* 31 May 1950; 12 June 1950; 3 March 1952; 4 March 1952.

Untitled newspaper clippings from unidentified newspapers. Geraldine L. Thompson personal file. 5 February 1931; 7 May 1931; 8 May 1931; 20 November 1952; 11 January 1953; n.d.

Woodbridge *News-Tribune.* 8 June 1972.

LETTERS AND NOTES

Babcock, Elisabeth T. Note attached to draft of speech of Geraldine L. Thompson.
Geraldine L. Thompson personal file, n.d.
———. Note attached to *National Geographic Magazine*'s special leaflet on the American
Museum of Natural History, Geraldine L. Thompson personal file, n.d.
———. Letters to Philip C. Carling, June 30, 1976; August 21, 1976.
———. Letter to Philip C. Carling, received August 31, 1976.
———. Letter to Mrs. Leigh Cook, March 28-31, 1974.
———. Letter to Dr. Ervin L. Harlacher, December 8, 1971.
———. Letters and notes to Linda Lott Rizzo, June 7, 1977; June 15, 1977; July 2,
1977; July 21, 1977.
Douglass, Dean Mabel S. Letter to Geraldine L. Thompson, May 6, 1931.
Harding, Charles B. Letter to Geraldine L. Thompson, November 13, 1963.
———. Letter to Geraldine L. Thompson, December 16, 1963.

Harlacher, Ervin L., first President of Brookdale Community College. Letter to Mary Lou Wagner, October 10, 1969.

Houston, Charles W. Letter to Geraldine L. Thompson, June 13, 1963.

Livengood, Winifred, Executive Director, Home Health Agency Assembly of New Jersey, Inc. Letter to Meline Karakashian, July 22, 1977.

McPhee, H. Roemer. Letter to Richard H. Pough, April 30, 1951.

Meyner, Governor Robert B. Letter to Geraldine L. Thompson, March 26, 1957.

Miller, Shirley, National Audubon Society. Postcard to Geraldine L. Thompson, n.d.

Mitchell, Mrs. Kenneth M., former President, Monmouth County Council, League of Women Voters. Letter to Monmouth County Board of Chosen Freeholders, file of Mrs. Josephine Lee, Red Bank.

Nilson, Carolyn. Taped letter to Joan Grantges, November 27, 1976.

———. Letter to Joan Grantges, December 19, 1976.

Pough, Richard H. Letter to Geraldine L. Thompson, March 29, 1951.

Thompson, Geraldine L. Letter to Dean Mabel S. Douglass, May 7, 1931.

———. Letter to "Helen" of the New York *Herald Tribune,* July 3, 1953.

———. Letter to Mrs. Lewis W. Jones, December 10, 1952.

———. Letter to Dr. Robert Nenno, November 27, 1963.

———. Letter to Geoffrey Parsons, June 1, 1951.

———. Letter to Carl A. Sheridan, August 15, 1952.

———. Letter to Commissioner John W. Tranburg, November 6, 1959.

———. Letter to Commissioner John W. Tranburg, November 13, 1959.

———. Letter to Lloyd Wescott, May 16, 1961.

Van Note, Dr. William G. Letter to Audrie LaTowsky, January 17, 1966.

INTERVIEWS

(Unless noted, interviews were conducted by AAUW committee members.)

Auch, Thomas H., Vice President and Treasurer, Brookdale Community College, and Shirley Zeisel, former Administrative Assistant to Mr. Auch. Lincroft, November 17, 1976.

Babcock, Elisabeth T. Interview conducted by Philip C. Carling, Woodbury, New York, August 25, 1976.

———. Lincroft, April 25, 1977

———. Telephone interview, Woodbury, New York, August 10, 1977.

Beadleston, State Senator Alfred N. Red Bank, November 23, 1976.

Bedell, State Senator Eugene J. Keansburg, December 1, 1976.

Bellin, Anita. Middletown, November 29, 1976.

Clark, Marvin A., former Trustee, Brookdale Community College, Freehold, November 11, 1976.

Clayton, Dr. Joseph E., former Superintendent of Monmouth County Schools, member of Board of Trustees, Brookdale Community College. West Belmar, December 1, 1976.

Clax, Anita. Lincroft, November 1, 1976.

Corderman, Major General W. Preston. Little Silver, January 23, 1976.

Danskin, Benjamin H., former member Monmouth County Board of Chosen Freeholders. Wall Township, December 17, 1976.

De Jong, Mrs. R. Tinton Falls, November 3, 1976.

Delehanty, Joan, and Barbara Niles. Monmouth Beach, November 15, 1976.

Ebeling, Elinor. Lincroft, December 2, 1976.

Fleckenstein, W.O., member of Board of Trustees, Brookdale Community College. Holmdel, January 25, 1977.

Fox, Carl V. Lincroft, November 9, 1976.

Garrison, Earl B., former Superintendent of Monmouth County Schools; Member of Board of Trustees, Brookdale Community College. Freehold, September 2, 1976.

Greene, James R., former Trustee, Brookdale Community College. Fair Haven, January 8, 1977.

Grigor, Helen O'Neill. Red Bank, November 9, 1976.

Harding, Charles B. Rumson, November 2, 1976.

Harding, Laura. Holmdel, November 9, 1976.

Harlacher, Dr. Ervin L., first President of Brookdale Community College. Speakerphone interview between Lincroft and Kansas City, Missouri, January 25, 1977.

Hazlett, Fred B. Lincroft, December 26, 1976.

Hoagland, Donald P. former Superintendent of Monmouth County Vocational School District. West Long Branch, December 1, 1976.

Holsey, Alan. Telephone interview. Sea Girt, March 16, 1977.

Holsey, Eleanor. Little Silver, April 6, 1977.

Irwin, Joseph C., former Director Monmouth County Board of Chosen Freeholders. Red Bank, September 20, 1976.

———. Telephone interview. Red Bank, January 19, 1977.

Kamin, Arthur Z., Editor, *The Daily Register.* Shrewsbury, December 10, 1976.

Kellenyi, Bernard. Red Bank, November 9, 1976.

Kelley, Elisabeth A. Lincroft, October 26, 1976.

Kelly, Madelyn Eagen. Lincroft, October, 1976.

LaTowsky, Audrie, former Vice-Chairman, Board of Trustees, Brookdale Community College. Wyckoff, New Jersey, August 11, 1976.

———. Middletown, November 2, 1976.

Lee, Josephine. Red Bank, February 22, 1977.

Leonard, Robert W., Dean of Community Services, Brookdale Community College. Lincroft, December 16, 1976.

Lilly, Mrs. Marshall. Telephone interviews. Lincroft, March, 1977.

Lubow, Lucille. Lincroft, November 10, 1976.

Manson, W. Gilbert. Red Bank, November 11, 1976.

Morgan, Charles L. Long Branch, October 28, 1976.

Mullin, Matthew, Jr. Telephone interview. Lincroft, March 23 and 24, 1977.

Mullin, Wilfred. Lincroft, November 4, 1976.

———. Telephone interview. Lincroft, March 23, 1977.

Multer, Elinor, former education writer, *Daily Register,* and former Director of Information Services, Brookdale Community College. Interview conducted by Philip C. Carling and Dr. Donald H. Smith. Lincroft, July 7, 1975.

Neidlinger, S. Travers. Leonardo, December 9, 1976.

Neuberger, Katherine, Chairman of New Jersey State Board of Higher Education. Lincroft, November 30, 1976.

Reilly, Edith, Executive Assistant, Brookdale Community College. Lincroft, December 9, 1976.

Sanderson, Elizabeth. Telephone interview. Little Silver, February 13, 1977.

Scheetz, Dr. Richard, New Jersey Department of Higher Education, 1958-1972. Lincroft,

August 25, 1976.

Smith, Dr. Donald H., President, Brookdale Community College. Lincroft, December 15 and 21, 1976.

Sterner, E. Donald, former New Jersey State Highway Commissioner. Belmar, January 26, 1977.

———. Telephone interview. Belmar, March 17, 1977.

Stout, Richard R., former State Senator. Allenhurst, November 1, 1976.

Stryker, Ella Kelly. Lincroft, October 1976.

Thompson, Martha, Media Specialist, Brookdale Community College. Lincroft, December 20, 1976.

Walsh, James. Neptune, December 1, 1976.

Wagner, Mary Lou. Lincroft, December 8, 1976.

White, Katharine Elkus, former United States Ambassador to Denmark, former Mayor of Red Bank. Red Bank, October 12, 1976.

Zar, Paul. Red Bank, December 9, 1977; telephone interview, Red Bank, January 9, 1977.

Zuckerman, Leon, Trustee, Brookdale Community College. Middletown, September 15, 1976.

The text of this book has been set in I.B.M. Composer font "Journal Roman" by Jet-Set Services, Matawan. The headings have been set in Alphatype font "English" by ABC Typography, Shrewsbury. The paper is Hopper Vellum Opaque, Natural, 50 lb. and the cover is Beckett Spanish Grain Duplex, Colonial Blue on White. The book was printed by Jersey Printing Company of Bayonne. The design is by Joan Longo and Barbara Maryanski.